A Brief History of Ancient Astrology

Brief Histories of the Ancient World

This new series offers concise, accessible, and lively accounts of central aspects of the ancient world. Each book is written by an acknowledged expert in the field and provides a compelling overview, for readers new to the subject and specialists alike.

Published
A Brief History of Ancient Astrology
Roger Beck

A Brief History of the Olympic Games
David C. Young

In Preparation
A Brief History of Ancient Greek
Stephen Colvin

A Brief History of Roman Law
Jill Harries

A Brief History of
Ancient Astrology

Roger Beck

Blackwell
Publishing

© 2007 by Roger Beck

BLACKWELL PUBLISHING
350 Main Street, Malden, MA 02148-5020, USA
9600 Garsington Road, Oxford OX4 2DQ, UK
550 Swanston Street, Carlton, Victoria 3053, Australia

First published 2007 by Blackwell Publishing Ltd

1   2007

Library of Congress Cataloging-in-Publication Data

Beck, Roger, 1937–
A brief history of ancient astrology / Roger Beck.
    p. cm. — (Brief histories of the ancient world)
Includes bibliographical references and index.
ISBN-13: 978-1-4051-1087-7 (hardback : alk. paper)
ISBN-10: 1-4051-1087-2 (hardback : alk. paper)
ISBN-13: 978-1-4051-1074-7 (pbk. : alk. paper)
ISBN-10: 1-4051-1074-0 (pbk. : alk. paper)
1. Astrology—History.   I. Title.   II. Series.
BF1674.B43 2007
133.5093—dc22   2006009414

A catalogue record for this title is available from the British Library.

Set in 10/13pt Minion
by SPi Publisher Services, Pondicherry, India
Printed and bound in Singapore
by Markono Print Media Pte Ltd

The publisher's policy is to use permanent paper from mills that operate a sustainable
forestry policy, and which has been manufactured from pulp processed using acid-free and
elementary chlorine-free practices. Furthermore, the publisher ensures that the text paper
and cover board used have met acceptable environmental accreditation standards.

For further information on
Blackwell Publishing, visit our website:
www.blackwellpublishing.com

For Janet

Contents

Figures

Tables

Preface

In setting out to write "a brief history of ancient astrology" I am in effect making four initial commitments. The first, brevity, will be easy enough to meet; and if I do not meet it myself, my editors will meet it for me. The third and fourth, defining the book's subject matter, "ancient astrology," are not very difficult either. "Antiquity," for our purposes, spans roughly the last century BCE and the first four centuries CE. *Classical* antiquity is intended: that is, the culture – or cultures – of the Mediterranean basin and Europe west of the Rhine and south of the Danube in the period indicated. Politically, that vast area was unified under Roman rule; culturally, it was diverse, but the predominant form was Greek, as was the language in which cultural forms were communicated. Thus "ancient astrology" means essentially "Greek astrology," although most of its practitioners and clients were not Greeks in any meaningful ethnic sense. Rome's empire, to its credit, was multi-ethnic and multi-cultural.

The problematic commitment is the second, offering a "history" of ancient astrology. Certainly one can construct narratives about aspects of ancient astrology. One can tell, in chronological sequence, the story of astrology's reception in its host culture, particularly in official Rome where episodes of exclusion alternated with periods of grudging acceptance and unofficial toleration. In fact this story has been told – and well told – by F. H. Cramer in *Astrology in Roman Law and Politics* (1954). Similarly, because horoscopes are datable, one can display and comment on the extant examples in chronological order as did O. Neugebauer and H. B. Van Hoesen in their magisterial compilation *Greek Horoscopes* (1959). Again, one can survey the extant astrological literature and trace the author-to-author flow of influence, as the Gundels did in their *Astrologumena* (1966). But to write a comprehensive history of ancient astrology as an art or technique that developed in a meaningful way over time would be a dubious undertaking. Changes no doubt occurred, though astrology was an unusually conservative art and indeed is still much the same today as it was in antiquity. But meaningful development implies progress, and by what standard can we measure progress in a pseudo-science? Overall, then, there is no satisfying narrative of ancient astrology to be told. There is simply no parallel to the story of the progressive mathematical refinement and enhanced predictive power of ancient astronomy.

Consequently, my "history" of ancient astrology will actually be something less ambitious, more in the nature of an *account* of various aspects of the subject, treated synchronically except where there is a tale to be told diachronically.

I have centered my account on the system itself, how horoscopes were constructed and interpreted. I have also chosen to dwell on actual examples, real horoscopes given and in some instances analyzed postmortem by the ancient experts themselves. Overall I have chosen depth and detail of example over breadth of coverage. To be comprehensive in the space allowed would be impossible, and the attempt at it would lead only to the superficial and uninteresting.

Inevitably scant justice or none at all will be done to some topics of secondary importance. The only one I need mention here is the ancient philosophical debate, focused mainly on the issue of fatalism, about astrology's value and validity. However, since this topic has been well handled by others, notably by A. A. Long in his article "Astrology: Arguments pro and contra" (1982), it will not be missed here.

Why would one devote a book to an account of a pseudo-science, long since invalidated? That is a question I should answer at the end of my presentation rather than the beginning. I shall however indicate as we go along some of the reasons why I think "just a pseudo-science" is a wholly inadequate characterization of ancient astrology.

1

Introduction. What Was Astrology in Ancient Greece and Rome?

1 Ancient Astronomy Versus Ancient Astrology: Some Misunderstandings

Modern studies of ancient astronomy and astrology tend to accentuate a dichotomy between the astronomy of antiquity as an emerging science and its astrology as a superstition whose only historic value was that it furnished a motive for investigating celestial regularities.

It is true that astrology, in the form in which it developed historically, could not have done so unaided by mathematical astronomy. To predict earthly "outcomes," as in a natal horoscope, one must know the positions of the stars and planets relative to each other and to the local horizon of the subject at the time of birth. Direct observation is obviously insufficient – births in daytime, cloud cover, phenomena below the horizon, unavailability of an astrologically qualified observer, and so on – and it was in fact seldom if ever used. Accordingly, ancient astrologers, like their modern successors, worked with tables, and the better the tables, the more accurate, so it seemed to the astrologers, must be their astrological predictions. It was of course the astronomers, or the astrologers themselves qua astronomers, who developed the mathematical models from which accurate tables, notably tables of planetary (including solar and lunar) longitudes, could be generated.

The history of science, precisely because its remit is the historic development of the scientific method and mentality, quite properly treats ancient astrology as a stage which astronomy outgrew, a necessary stage perhaps, but in the longer term an embarrassment to be discarded. While I will of course respect the scientific distinction between astronomical fact and astrological fantasy, I will not be overly concerned with it. As a historian of astrology my remit is cultural and intellectual history, in particular how the Greeks and Romans searched for meaning and significance in the phenomena of the visible heavens. I do not deny that the significance sought in the astrological domain was entirely non-scientific. But within my frame of reference, that is not a very interesting fact: astrological predictions don't work; *quid novi*, so what else is new?

The dichotomizing paradigm of the history of science (astronomy good, astrology bad) has hampered the study of ancient astrology in three unfortunate ways.[1] Firstly, in its disdain for astrology and astrologers the dominant modern paradigm trivializes the object of study, seldom a healthy or fruitful approach. If superstition is all you expect to find, superstition is probably all you will in fact find. The ancient astrological handbooks do indeed contain, from the scientific perspective, vast reams of nonsense. However, the mentality behind this nonsense was by no means unsubtle and unsophisticated; and in any case constructs of empirical nonsense are not infrequently among the more interesting products of human culture. My quarrel is not with the history of science in its proper domain but with triumphalist scientism rampant beyond it.

Secondly, the modern approach takes little account of the dominant ancient paradigm, well exemplified in the introductions to Ptolemy's astronomical and astrological treatises (respectively, the *Almagest* and the *Tetrabiblos*), which treated the two disciplines as a single predictive enterprise, of greater or lesser certitude, searching for regularities and significance in the motions and positions of the celestial bodies. The

2

modern scientist is not of course constrained by ancient paradigms, but the historian of the ancient mentality most certainly is – constrained by, though not confined to.

Thirdly and most insidiously, the modern dichotomizing approach, in separating astronomical gold from astrological slag, treats the "slag" too uniformly as consisting entirely of technical, predictive astrology. This approach is understandable, for the extant astrological literature and horoscopes are almost all oriented to that end: human "outcomes" predicted on the basis of celestial configurations. Nevertheless, there is some warrant in the ancient data for extending the working definition of astrology to include the search for metaphysical and theological meaning in the stars. Much of the data lies in astral symbolism within religious contexts, in particular data from the Mysteries of Mithras, a cult whose astronomy and astrology have long been at the focus of my research (Beck 2004, 2006). A recognition of ancient astrology's wider domain and significance is one of my major goals. Accordingly, I intend this book as a contribution to the cultural and intellectual history of classical antiquity, not just a self-contained history of the art and practice of astrology over a certain time period.

2 Demarcation: Ptolemy on the Remits of Astronomy and Astrology

Did the ancients themselves, specifically the Greeks, distinguish between two different approaches to celestial phenomena, an astronomical approach and an astrological approach, as we would term them? Yes, they did, and many of them did so on commonsensical criteria which we still apply today: the predictions of astronomers can be trusted; those of astrologers, when you can pin them down, cannot be.

Notice that I do not speak of a discrimination between the true and the false, the real and the unreal, the scientific and the unscientific, between facts which are empirically verifiable and unverifiable nonsense. To do so would beg all sorts of questions, principally about the nature of "science" and the paradigms of it which successive ages hold implicitly or explicitly. So rather than treating "scientific" astronomy as an unvarying given and characterizing astrology simply as an aberration there from, let us also ask some questions about astronomy in classical antiquity, in particular how its own practitioners construed the discipline.

Only a single major work of ancient Greek astronomy has been preserved for us in its entirety – Ptolemy's *Almagest*, composed in about CE 150 (trans. Toomer 1984). No one doubts that it was the best and most comprehensive in the field. In its preface (*Alm.* 1.1) Ptolemy is at pains to define his discipline and to relate it to other disciplines. Now Ptolemy subsequently wrote a treatise on astrology known from its four parts or "books" as the *Tetrabiblos* (trans. Robbins 1971). Whether it too was the best in its field is today unanswerable, not because there are no other extant treatises to compare it with – there are, some of which we shall meet later – but because meaningful criteria for "best in show" when the show is astrology cannot now be formulated. More to the point, though, Ptolemy is just as concerned with defining astrology in the *Tetrabiblos* (1.1) as he is with defining astronomy in the *Almagest*, adding moreover chapters on whether "astrological knowledge is attainable" and if attainable whether it is also "helpful" (1.2–3). By comparing the beginnings of these two treatises, we can thus recapture the relationship between astronomy and astrology as seen by a scientist who was both the pre-eminent practitioner of the former and a leading theoretician of the latter. One could not hope for better, provided of course that Ptolemy was broadly in tune with the intellectual spirit of his times – which he most certainly was.

Let us start with astronomy and the *Almagest* (1.1). Among what we would call the arts and sciences and the Greeks the divisions of "philosophy," astronomy, says Ptolemy, is a branch of one of the three forms of "theoretical" (as opposed to "practical") philosophy. The three forms of theoretical philosophy are (1) theology, which is concerned with immutable and imperceptible objects, (2) mathematics, which is concerned with immutable but perceptible objects, and (3) physics, which is concerned with mutable and perceptible objects. Astronomy belongs to the intermediate form, mathematics, because its objects of study, the stars and planets, meet the two necessary conditions of immutability and perceptibility. What is mutable, Ptolemy asserts, cannot be surely known; likewise neither can that which is entirely beyond perception. Because astronomy, qua mathematical philosophy, studies objects which are both perceptible and immutable, it is an excellent road to knowledge, the best as Ptolemy sees it.

Certainly, the premise that what cannot be perceived cannot be known makes a good deal of sense, especially if we think of knowledge in terms of the acquisition of verifiable truths about the world. But why can there be no knowledge of mutable things? Ptolemy seems to be excluding just about everything we would consider the proper objects of scientific inquiry – except the stars, which from a modern point of view are no less mutable than any other class of objects in the perceptible universe.

Here we must confront the – to us – massively alien postulates on which Ptolemy founds the science of astronomy. Like virtually all intellectuals in classical antiquity Ptolemy thought in terms of order, rank, and hierarchy. In any category you care to name, some things were simply superior to, better than, others. Ontologically, the permanent trumps the impermanent, the abstract trumps the concrete, the simple and uniform trump the complex. Epistemically, to comprehend something permanent trumps the comprehension of something mutable, so much so that only the former really qualifies as "knowledge."

For permanency nothing in the perceptible universe beats the celestial bodies. Since all changes to their appearances (the phases of the Moon, eclipse phenomena, the reddening of the sun as it rises from or sinks below the horizon) can be readily explained by external causes, the conclusion that the stars themselves are unchanging in their nature was hard to avoid. So if unchanging, then immortal; and if immortal, then divine.

Although the stars do not seem to change in and of themselves, they most certainly change position, both collectively in the apparent rotation of the universe around our globe of earth, and in the case of the sun, the moon, and the other five planets visible to the naked eye, relative to each other and the "fixed" stars, in highly complex patterns of individual motion.

Accordingly, Greek astronomy concerned itself exclusively with *motion*, that is with change of *position* over *time*. As Ptolemy put it, "that division [of theoretical philosophy] which determines the nature involved in forms and motion from place to place, and which serves to investigate shape, number, size, and place, time and suchlike, one may define as 'mathematics' " (*Alm.* 1.1, trans. Toomer).

Note that Ptolemy's definition covers, as it must, geometry and arithmetic ("mathematics" in the modern sense) as well astronomy. Note also how Ptolemy defines the lowest – not his word, but a fair reflection of his attitude, I think – division of theoretical philosophy: "The division [of theoretical philosophy] which investigates material and ever-moving nature, and which concerns itself with 'white', 'hot', 'sweet', 'soft' and suchlike qualities one may call 'physics'; such an order of being is situated (for the most part) amongst corruptible bodies and below the lunar sphere" (*Alm.* 1.1, trans. Toomer).

The distinction between the "sublunary" world of "corruptible bodies" and the celestial world of the permanent and divine was reinforced by Aristotle's differentiation between the motion proper to bodies in each realm. Observation and common sense suggest that things on earth move in a straight line up or down unless impetus in some other direction, whose cause we can see, is imparted to them. They do not, of their own accord, move in circles. But that, the Greeks discovered, was precisely what the celestial bodies do or appear to do: they revolve in orbits around the earth, all of them together westward in the period of a day, and the seven planets eastward (for the most part) in different periods and complex individual orbits. It follows then that celestial bodies differ from terrestrial not only in durability but also fundamentally in their very nature: they are endowed with the alien quality of autonomous circular motion. Not until Newton and the discovery of the universal applicability of the laws of gravity was this great conceptual gulf between earth and heaven bridged: stuff "up there" is the same as stuff "down here."

Even on modern criteria the *Almagest* is indisputably a work of science. It makes no statements about the motions, positions, and periods of the celestial bodies which cannot be verified or falsified.

But we would do well to remember that it is not a secular work: it is a work about the behavior of visible gods, and for that reason Ptolemy quite properly locates it midway between theology (immortal and imperceptible objects) and physics (mortal and perceptible objects) as a discipline concerned with the very special class of objects which though immortal are nevertheless perceptible and hence scientifically comprehensible.

And the practical utility of astronomy? That too is as theological as it is ethical. "With regard to virtuous conduct in practical actions and character, this science, above all things, could make men see clearly; from the constancy, order, symmetry and calm which are associated with the divine, it makes its followers lovers of this divine beauty, accustoming them and reforming their natures, as it were, to a similar spiritual state" (*Alm.* 1.1, trans. Toomer).

Ptolemy introduces his later work, the *Tetrabiblos*, as a companion piece, a sequel to the *Almagest*. Astrology for Ptolemy is not a separate discipline from astronomy, and it is certainly not an unscientific application of astronomy. It is simply part two of "prognosis through astronomy" (*Tetr.* 1.1, first sentence). Notice how he does not even give astrology a technical name of its own:[2]

> Of the means of prediction through astronomy, O Syrus, two are the most important and valid. One, which is first both in order and effectiveness, is that whereby we apprehend the aspects of the movements of sun, moon, and stars in relation to each other and to the earth, as they occur from time to time; the second is that in which by means of the natural character of these aspects themselves we investigate the changes which they bring about in that which they surround [i.e. the earth]. (*Tetr.* 1.1, trans. Robbins)

The first method, Ptolemy reminds his patron Syrus, he has already expounded in the treatise we know as the *Almagest*. It enables us to predict the positions of the celestial bodies relative to each other and the earth through knowledge of their orbital motions. By the second method we examine the "configurations" (*schêmatismous*) of the heavenly bodies to predict the changes which the celestial configurations effect on earth through their "natural qualities."

In judging the second method, says Ptolemy, there are two errors to avoid. The first is to suppose that one can attain the level of "certainty" reached by the first method. That is an impossible goal because the second method addresses our mutable world of "material quality," where things can only be "guessed at" – and that "with difficulty" (the single word *dyseikaston*). The second error is to go to the other extreme and deny the possibility of drawing any true and useful conclusions about the effects of the celestial on the terrestrial, which is to fly in the face of the evidence of manifest celestial causation such as the sun's daily and annual effects on earth.

The plausibility of Ptolemy's argument from solar influence to the influence of celestial bodies in general does not yet concern us, for our task in this first chapter has only been to differentiate between astronomy and astrology as the ancient Greeks conceived the two enterprises. Taking Ptolemy as our guide, we have seen how an expert in both might integrate them as a single predictive art yielding results of greater or lesser probability and reliability.

2

Origins and Types of Astrology. The Transfer of Astrology from Babylon. The Pseudo-History of Astrology: "Alien Wisdom"

1 Types of Astrology

The dominant form of Greek astrology, current throughout the Roman empire, was genethlialogy. The word is unfamiliar, but both in theory and in practice the thing itself was much the same as standard horoscopic astrology today.

Genethlialogy means the science of "births." It focuses on the celestial configurations at the time of a subject's birth or, more rarely, conception (assumed to be nine months prior to birth if not otherwise known). It claims to foretell an individual's fate, fortunes, and character on the basis of those configurations. Thus, what we call a horoscope is essentially what the Greeks called a nativity (*genesis*). Many original horoscopes have been recovered from the ancient world (most of them on scraps of papyrus preserved in the dry sands of Egypt), and some were also recorded as case studies in astrological handbooks which are still extant. The handbooks themselves were mostly concerned with genethlialogy or, as they termed them, "outcomes" (*apotelesmata*): if configuration X at birth, then outcome Y in life.

Of the other forms of astrology practiced by the ancients,[1] general astrology applies the methods of genethlialogy to collectives (peoples, cities, and so on) rather than individuals. Catarchic astrology, so called from a Greek word meaning "beginning," looks for the astrologically opportune moment to launch an enterprise. Catarchic astrology turns genethlialogy back to front, as it were. Instead of arguing from a given configuration to a probable outcome, catarchic astrology argues from a desired outcome to the configuration most likely to bring about that outcome.

Interrogatory astrology answers questions with reference to the current configuration of the heavens. The ubiquitous astrological columns of newspapers are of this type. Since a single prediction would both strain credibility and offend the reader's sense of individuality – how can one size possibly fit all? – these columns throw in a variable: the outcome of today's configuration depends on the sign of the zodiac in which the sun stood on the day of your birth. To determine this, all you need to know is the day and month of your birth (the year is irrelevant) and from that you can determine your "sun sign." Born on January 11, I for example am "a Capricorn." Twelve sizes, not one, fit all.

The oldest form of astrology is what we call omen astrology. Its persistence in Greek astrology, albeit in a very minor role, reveals the dependence of Greek astrology on Babylonian astrology. The former, as we shall see, is the latter's progeny. What distinguishes omen astrology from horoscopic astrology is the absence of a comprehensive system relating all actual and potential celestial configurations on a single grid. Horoscopic astrology treats of the positions of the celestial bodies relative to each other and to the earth. As we saw in chapter 1, it is the "aspects" of the stars and planets, not the stars and planets themselves, that indicate or determine outcomes. Omen astrology deals primarily with discrete and occasional phenomena, especially dramatic ones such as eclipses; and since the ancients could not differentiate on scientific grounds between what happens in "space" and what happens in earth's own atmosphere, omen astrology included meteorological indicators, thunder in particular, with celestial phenomena proper.

As an example of Greek omen astrology I quote from a text preserved in an agricultural treatise, the *Geoponica* (1.10).[2] (The text claims to be by the Persian prophet Zoroaster but is certainly not!)

> Indication of outcomes from the first thunder each year after the rising of Sirius. From Zoroaster. The thunder which occurs after the rising of Sirius should be considered the first of each year. One must observe in what house [i.e. sign] of the zodiac the Moon is when first thunder occurs. If first thunder occurs when the Moon is in Aries, it indicates that certain people in the land will be incited to unrest and that strife and mass flight will take place but that later there will be a settlement. If first thunder occurs when the Moon is in Taurus, it indicates that there will be crop losses of wheat and barley, and an onslaught of locusts; happiness in the royal court, but oppression and famine among those in the east. [And so on through the remaining ten signs.]

Would that prediction in politics, agriculture, and economics were that simple (though one wonders what the government would be so happy about in the second instance)!

Note how the omen itself, thunder, is particularized. This is not just any old clap of thunder, it is the first thunder of the year. How does one define first? First means the first to occur after the rising of Sirius, the Dog Star. By "rising" the "heliacal" rising is intended, the day on which for the first time in the year Sirius can be observed in the pre-dawn twilight rising ahead of the Sun (on the day before, it would still have been too close to the Sun to be seen). Depending on latitude, that date fell in late July or very early August.

"First thunder," though, does not indicate a single outcome. A variable is introduced which yields radically different outcomes. That variable is the position of the Moon in the signs of the zodiac. Bear in mind that the Moon moves (eastward) very quickly, completing a full circuit of the signs in some twenty-seven and one third days. So it traverses each sign in about two-and-one-quarter days. Between one day and the next that thunder clap can change its meaning from revolution to famine.

2 Out of Babylon

Greek omen astrology takes us back to astrology's origins in Babylon, whether or not any particular Greek text originated there. The types of outcome indicated by the thunder signs quoted above are very similar to those found in the records of Babylonian omen astrology dating back into the second millennium BCE.[3] The eventualities foretold in Babylonian omen astrology are overwhelmingly in the public domain or (what amounts to the same thing) in the royal domain: war and peace, rebellion and tranquility, good crops and plenty, poor crops and famine. Which brings us to the Babylonian astrologers — the watchers, recorders, analysts, and calculators who observed the heavens, interpreted the data, and tried to discern and express mathematically the regularities by which the Sun, Moon, and planets change position over time.

The Babylonian astrologers were civil servants with a job to do, to advise the authorities on what the visible gods in heaven intended for the state on earth and foretold by their comings and goings and encounters one with another. The more one knows about the regularities and repetitions of celestial motion, the further ahead and the more accurately one can predict planetary positions and encounters. So from professional necessity astrologers developed as astronomers. This is not to deny that disinterested curiosity, what we would call the spirit of scientific inquiry, at some stage entered the Babylonian astral enterprise. Their astronomical achievements were too advanced, too mathematically precise, too far beyond the mere requirements of guild competence, to suppose otherwise.

Although not a part of astrology in the narrow modern sense, another function of the Babylonian astral bureaucrats must be mentioned, since it concerns their motivation. That function was the regulation of the calendar. Getting control of time has always been a reason for studying the stars, particularly the Sun and the Moon; for time is measured by those two bodies, the day and the year by the Sun, and the month by the Moon. As well as the inherent desirability of a reliable civil calendar – how can you pay the rent "on time" if you and your landlord do not know what "on time" is? – there is another motive for getting it right: the good will of the gods, who will be seriously displeased if through ignorance you celebrate their festivals on the wrong day.

Fixing the calendar is by no means straightforward, and it was especially difficult for those like the Babylonians and most other ancient peoples who reckoned by true lunar months, that is by actual cycles of the Moon's phases, from the first appearance of the lunar crescent in the evening ("new moon") through "full moon" and back again to first appearance. There are two major problems, both of which the Babylonians eventually solved. Firstly, *predicting* the Moon's first appearance and thus the beginning of the month involves manipulating mathematically a very large array of variables which the astronomers must first isolate and analyze. Secondly, twelve lunar months fall short of the solar year by approximately eleven days. Consequently, if you wish to keep the twelve lunar months each more or less in its proper seasonal place in the solar year, you have to add at fairly frequent intervals a thirteenth "intercalary" month. Throwing in the extra month ad hoc is a poor solution for a civil calendar. Rather, one needs a reliable formula for intercalation in set years in a cycle which repeats itself indefinitely into the future. The solution was found in the nineteen-year "Metonic" cycle applied systematically in Babylon in the civil calendar in the early fourth-century BCE (at the latest). From the realization that nineteen solar years are approximately the same in duration as 235 lunar ("synodic") months, the Babylonians were able to put in place a true and reasonably accurate luni-solar calendar by intercalation of seven additional months at set intervals in a cycle of nineteen years.[4]

Babylon's astronomical heyday, from a scientific perspective, came late, not until the last three centuries BCE, when the country was under foreign rule (when not?), first of Alexander the Great's general Seleucus and his successors and then of the Parthians, an Iranian people. The records of the astral bureaucracy were archived on sun-baked clay tablets, which is why so many of them have been preserved, though in fragments more often than not. Historians of astronomy have divided them into two broad groups: (1) "mathematical," the majority of which are "ephemerides" giving in effect the distances to be traveled each day by the Sun, the Moon, and the other five planets so that you can foretell who will be where when; and (2) "nonmathematical," the majority of which are "diaries" telling you retrospectively, along with many other data, who was where when.[5] Omen astrology does not fit into this taxonomy, which is of course ours, not theirs. It was the first on the scene and is best exemplified in the multi-tablet series *Enuma Anu Enlil*, a compilation of the seventh century BCE which drew on material as much as a thousand years older. There is no need to quote an example in addition to that already quoted from pseudo-Zoroaster many centuries later. In form, contents, and function there is no significant difference between the Greek form of omen astrology and the Babylonian form from which the Greek descended.[6]

A small proportion of the recovered "nonmathematical" texts consists of horoscopes.[7] That these texts are truly horoscopes in the technical sense is beyond question, for they explicitly link a birth with astronomical data pertaining on the date of birth. Foremost among those data are the longitudes of the seven planets, principally the Sun and the Moon, expressed in terms of the sign and the degree of the sign then occupied by the planet in question. Here then are the indisputable origins of genethlialogy. The earliest of the texts dates to 410 BCE, the latest to 69 BCE, with the bulk of them falling in the third and second centuries.

Very little more can be said with certainty about Babylonian genethlialogy, except that it is a product of the same astral bureaucracy that produced the full range of astronomical texts both mathematical and nonmathematical. While one can plausibly claim on the grounds of relative chronology that the requirements of the old form of omen astrology gave an initial impetus to the development of scientific astronomy in Babylon, the same cannot be said of genethlialogy.

14

The tail of horoscopy manifestly did not wag the astronomical dog. To change the metaphor, genethlialogy was a spin-off of Babylonian astronomy as it entered its prime.

What is clear is that Babylonian horoscopes were constructed retrospectively from records, not by direct observation of the heavens at the time of birth. Demonstrably, they drew on the diaries, for they frequently include data from those very sources, for example lunar data for the month of birth, dates and particulars of eclipses before or after, and dates of the nearest solstice or equinox. Astronomically, the standard Babylonian horoscope is richer and more informative than the standard non-literary Greek horoscope.

Of the "natives" of the horoscopes we know nothing, other than a few names (two of them Greek, incidentally); and while outcomes are sometimes included, they are expressed in rather general terms. At any rate, there is little in the horoscopes so far discovered to indicate elaborate and precise systems correlating celestial causes with outcomes in the lives of the natives. Interestingly, almost all of the Greek horoscopes other than those embedded in literary sources have no outcomes either.

3 Via Egypt

Sometime during the Hellenistic age, probably in the third or second centuries BCE, both mathematical astronomy and genethlialogy migrated westward from Babylon to the Greek world of the eastern Mediterranean. The Hellenistic age was the period, coinciding roughly with the last three centuries BCE, when the old Persian empire, conquered by Alexander the Great, was ruled by his successors – notably the Seleucids in Syria and Mesopotamia and the Ptolemies in Egypt – and the entire "Near East," as we would call it, became accessible to Greek culture. As the age wore on, Mesopotamia was recovered by the Parthians and Rome's empire encroached from the west, until with the collapse of Cleopatra's Egypt, Graeco-Macedonian political control of that whole vast area was finally extinguished. But not Greek culture; nor for that matter the vibrant native cultures which flourished alongside the Greek. Of those cultures the most important in the history of astrology was the Egyptian.

Because of the relative ease of communications the early Hellenistic age afforded the best, perhaps the only, opportunity in antiquity for the transfer of precise astronomical knowledge from east to west. Either one or more easterners came west with that knowledge, or else one or more westerners went east and then returned with it; or perhaps knowledge flowed westward in the minds and baggage of both easterners and westerners.

At the highest scientific level, the presence of Babylonian mathematical astronomy is evident in the work of the great Hipparchus (active ca. 150–125 BCE). Indeed it is central to his entire project, which was to render the geometric models of Greek astronomy more credible by endowing them with greater predictive accuracy. In Hipparchus' day only the Babylonian arithmetical schemes and observational records could furnish the required precision. The current view is that one or more Greeks "having considerable technical competence," perhaps even Hipparchus himself, "extracted reports from the archive with the collaboration of the astronomers of Babylon."[8]

The indebtedness of the high Greek tradition to Babylonian astronomy has been known for over a century. Much more recent is the discovery, thanks mostly to the work of Alexander Jones (1991, 1999a, 1999b), that a rich repertoire of Babylonian predictive astronomy entered Egypt in the Hellenistic age and was cultivated there independently of any high tradition. The primary function of this Greco-Egyptian mathematical astronomy, as we shall see more clearly in the next chapter, was to service genethlialogical astrology, for horoscopes appear in the record at roughly the same time. Unlike the clay tablets of Babylon, the record in Egypt consists of scraps of papyrus and ostraka (fragments of pottery recycled as writing surfaces). Most of these documents postdate the beginning of the common era (1 CE), and there may well have been something of a boom in genethlialogy and its astronomical "tech support" in the Egypt of the early Roman empire. However, the paucity of earlier records is not a reliable index of fashion, still less of date of origin, having more to do with contingent factors of preservation, for example the height of a water table below which older papyrus records would have rotted away. We can be confident that genethlialogy and its astronomical support were up and running in Egypt in the first century BCE, if not already in the second.

4 Pseudo-Histories

The older the better. Age, until modern times, was always the badge of legitimacy and authority. So, strangely enough, for the Greeks was foreign origin. The Greeks were aware that compared with the cultures of the ancient Near East theirs was a young culture much indebted to "alien wisdom."[9] To be sure, they were quite capable of cultural chauvinism – less so of out-and-out racism, since being "Greek" was not so much a matter of ethnicity as of speaking the language and assimilating oneself to the culture. Nevertheless, respect for other cultures and their legendary sages ran deep in the Greek philosophical tradition. If there was a perverse side to this respect, it was the readiness of admiring Greeks to pass off their own works as that of the alien sages, not so much with the intent to deceive as to place themselves within an admired tradition. The omen astrology of "Zoroaster" quoted earlier in this chapter is a case in point.[10]

For astrology there was good reason to write up both its antiquity and its foreign provenance, for it is a fact that the Greeks had access to precise astronomical records going back to the eighth century BCE,[11] just as it is a fact that astrology together with arithmetical astronomy came from external cultures, the Babylonian and the Egyptian, though of course the Egypt which transmitted astrology and its supportive astronomy was as Greek as it was native Egyptian.

For those who dealt in antique wisdom, however, mere centuries were insufficient. If "Zoroaster" could be pushed back five or six millennia,[12] still more impressive numbers were surely warranted for the "Chaldeans," as the ancient astrologers of Mesopotamia were called. Figures of half a million years and more were postulated.[13] However, it is only fair to say that such figures were treated with skepticism by intellectuals who had no interest vested in the antiquity of astrological record-keeping. Skeptics made the shrewd point that though records of earlier ages would indeed be useful, especially of previous cycles of planetary motion which were now being repeated with the same day-by-day configurations, the time spans of such repetitions (or "great years") were simply too vast for continuous record-keeping.[14] No one, more-over, was coming forward with actual records from the last time round.[15]

We have already seen a specimen of the astrological learning falsely attributed to the Persian prophet Zoroaster. But the figures who emerged as the putative founders and arch-authorities of astrology were Egyptian; Nechepso the king and Petosiris the priest. (So great an enterprise needs regal power as well as sacred wisdom at its incep-tion.) There may have been historical persons behind these two authors, as there was of course behind "Zoroaster," but if so they certainly did not compose the works attributed to them. These works, which survive only in fragments and which in any case were more a medley of texts coagulating around a pair of authoritative names rather than a single coauthored set of books, consist of a mass of omen astrology, geneth-lialogy, medical astrology ("iatromathematics"), and botanical and mineralogical astrology, in other words astral lore connected with plants and stones.[16] The collection of material cannot be precisely dated since it grew by accumulation over time, but the consensus is that it formed in the second half of the second century BCE and/or the first century BCE. It is the oldest corpus of Greek astrological literature, but that does not mean that it was in any sense the foundation text of actual Greek astrology.

The works of Nechepso and Petosiris belong to that large body of Graeco-Egyptian writing on arcane topics, both magical and religious, which we call "Hermetic," because of the ultimate attribution of many of its texts to a revelation of the god Hermes (styled Trismegistus, the "thrice-greatest") who was equated with the Egyptian Thoth as the god of learning and its transmission.[17] Within this tradition falls a herbal ("On the Virtue of Plants") attributed to one Thessalus and prefaced by an autobiographical letter to a first-century CE Roman emperor. The letter-writer explains how as an eager young iatromathematician he had tried to put into practice the methods of Nechepso which he had discovered in a treatise chanced upon in a library. The result: complete failure and embarrassment. In desperation he went in search of an explanation from the gods and was finally rewarded with a theophany of the healing god (and frequent player in Hermeticism) Asclepius. Asclepius explains that Nechepso, "though a wise man possessed of great magical powers," had got it only half right: "...he had grasped the affinities of stones and plants with the stars, but he did not know the times or places where the plants must be gathered." The story is interesting for what it tells about ancient perceptions of hierarchies of arcane knowledge and the rhetoric and narratives by which one legitimated both knowledge and professional craft.[18]

3

The Product: How to Construct a Simple Horoscope, Ancient Style

1 The Geometry of the Zodiac: Aspects

A Greek horoscope closely resembles a Babylonian horoscope in astronomical data: principally, they both give the positions of the planets, expressed in terms of the signs of the zodiac then occupied, at the time of birth. But behind the Greek horoscopes there lurks a huge change in cosmological thinking. We have entered a world of geometry to which the Babylonian world of arithmetic is subservient.

For Ptolemy as an astrologer, you will remember (chapter 1), it was not the stars themselves or even the stars in particular positions that were of paramount importance, but the "aspects" of the stars to each other and to the earth. The aspects are geometrical relationships, and the geometry involved is the elementary geometry of a circle when you divide its circumference into twelve equal sectors.

Figure 3.1 shows the circle of the zodiac divided into the twelve equal signs. Strictly speaking, the circle itself is the ecliptic, which is the annual path of the Sun, while the zodiac is a band of the heavens, some 12° in width, of which the ecliptic is the median line. By convention the circle

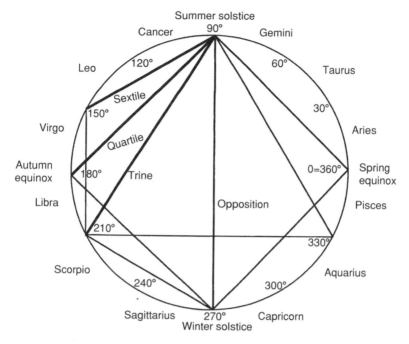

Figure 3.1 The circle of the zodiac and the aspects

was deemed to start at the beginning of Aries, which is thus the first of the signs. The signs are counted in the order in which the Sun passes through them in his annual journey, so the second sign is Taurus, the third Gemini, and so on round to Pisces as the twelfth. The sequence in figure 3.1 thus runs counter-clockwise.

The *signs* of the zodiac are not the same as the *constellations* whose names they share. Constellations are groups of stars; the signs, as explained above, are geometrical constructs. Of course when first constructed the signs did more or less coincide with the constellations from which they were named. But a phenomenon, discovered by Hipparchus and known as the "precession of the equinoxes," has caused them to drift slowly apart, with the result that the sign of Aries now coincides with the stars Pisces and the sign of Taurus with the stars of Aries. This

21

poses a problem for modern astrologers (whence the influence, from the sign or the constellation?), but although precession and its long-term effects and implications were known to ancient astronomers and to a few astrologers, the uncoupling of signs and constellations could still be ignored in practice.

The convention which makes Aries the first of the signs is tantamount to a decision to begin the year in the spring. For Aries was and is the sign where the Sun crosses the celestial equator from south to north bringing the season when day becomes longer than night. In both space and time this point is the vernal or spring equinox. Although Babylonian variants which placed the spring equinox at Aries $8°$ or $10°$ persisted for some time in Greek astrology, the Greek convention which placed it at the beginning of the sign eventually prevailed, as it did in Greek astronomy and as it does today. Figure 3.1 shows this point on the right side of the circle, at 3 o'clock.

To return to the "aspects" with which we began, the geometry of the circle of twelve equal sectors determines that a planet which, for example, is at the start of Cancer (longitude $90°$) is in opposition or diametrical aspect to a planet at the start of Capricorn ($270°$), in trine aspect to a planet at the start of Scorpio ($210°$), in quartile aspect to a planet at the start of Libra ($180°$), and in sextile aspect to a planet at the start of Virgo ($150°$). As figure 3.1 shows, three planets in trine aspect to one another form a triangle within the circle of the zodiac, four in quartile aspect form a square, and six in sextile aspect a hexagon. Any significance imputed by astrologers to these aspects (for example, trine generally favorable, quartile unfavorable) does not yet concern us. For the moment we are dealing only with (a) the actualities of celestial appearances – there really is an ecliptic, a great circle on the celestial sphere round which the Sun appears to travel in the course of the year – and (b) the necessary, definitional truths of geometry: for example, an equilateral triangle is formed by connecting three points at intervals of $120°$.

In the opening sentences of the *Tetrabiblos* (quoted in chapter 1) Ptolemy speaks of the aspects of the celestial bodies not only to each other but also to the earth. In fact the aspects described above include the earth by definition. Two planets in trine aspects, for example, are separated by an arc of 120° on the circumference of the circle of the ecliptic. The same fact can be stated by saying that the two planets subtend an angle of 120° at the point-sized central earth. Including the earth in these relationships is essential, for astrology as a would-be practical art is all about relating the things of heaven to the things on earth. That the Greeks and Romans placed the earth at the center of the universe is well known, as for the most part is the fact that they conceived of it as a sphere. Less well known is the fact that the astronomers, at least, were well aware that relative to the universe the earth is a mere dimensionless point (as demonstrated by Ptolemy at *Alm.* 1.6). In a formal sense the geometry of aspects properly treats the negligible size of the earth as axiomatic.

2 The Planets "in" the Signs

From the necessary truths of geometry we move to contingent celestial facts. The primary data of astrology are the positions of the seven planets in the signs of the zodiac (in genethlialogy, at the time of the "native's" birth). Imagine the circle of the zodiac as the circle of hours on a clock-face: twelve signs, twelve hours. Now imagine that the clock has not two but seven hands, each of which by its movements indicates the changing positions of its planet as it passes from sign to sign. Using figure 3.1 as our clock-face, we must imagine these seven planetary hands sweeping round in a counter-clockwise direction (with occasional reversals to be mentioned below).

The Moon completes her circuit in a month, though the month in question, the "tropical" month,[1] is about two days shorter than what we usually think of as a month, that is the period of time between one "new moon" and the next. The latter is the "synodic" month and it is longer than the tropical month because the Moon needs the additional time to catch up with the Sun which is also on the move. The synodic month is completed when the Moon once again reaches conjunction with the Sun, when her clock-hand and his "tell the same time," as it were. The Sun of course takes a year to complete his circuit. Neither the Sun nor the Moon moves at a uniform speed. Their hands, in other words, are

23

sometimes ahead of and sometimes behind the points they would occupy were they turning at uniform speed.

The other five planets move even more erratically, indeed so erratically that they occasionally slow to a stop and reverse direction. When they have completed their "retrograde" (backwards) arcs, they again slow to a stop and then resume forward motion.[2] Mercury and Venus complete their circuits in a year on average. These are the two "inferior" planets, so called because in the ancient geocentric system they are the planets closer to earth than the Sun and so "below" him as one moves "up" from earth to heaven. In appearance the inferior planets are the close attendants of the Sun in his annual progress around the signs. Mercury is never more than one sign away from the Sun and Venus never more than two. Consequently they are only observable either in the sky to the west after sunset or to the east before sunrise. Frequently they are too close to the Sun to be visible at all, and glimpses of Mercury are in fact quite rare. "Above" the Sun are the three "superior" planets, Mars, Jupiter, and Saturn. They are not tied to the Sun as are their "inferior" colleagues, so you will find them, at some time or another, in every aspect to, or "elongation" from, the Sun. When in opposition to the Sun, they are always in retrograde motion. The periods of the superior planets, roughly speaking, are two years for Mars, twelve for Jupiter, and thirty for Saturn.

The positions of the planets in the signs are facts. Accordingly one can make verifiably true statements about them. Thus, if today I say that Venus is in Taurus I am making a claim which you can verify by observation or by reference to an ephemeris or to a table of planetary motions. My claim is true if and only if Venus actually is in Taurus; otherwise it is false. The two little words "is in" carry a good deal of freight, but fortunately you and I agree about their intent (or we would not be having this conversation). We agree that we are talking about the current position ("in Taurus") of a certain point source of light (Venus). Technically, we mean that Venus (so intended) is – or is not – somewhere between longitude 30° (the beginning of Taurus) and longitude 60° (the end of Taurus and the beginning of Gemini). Note that our "truths" are the truths of *appearances*. Put another way, they are the truths of *positional* astronomy only.

Clearly, the statement "Venus is now in Taurus," if true, is true in a very different sense from the statement "a celestial body in Taurus is in trine aspect to a celestial body in Virgo." The latter is true necessarily and by definition – it cannot be otherwise – while the former is true only as long as the planet Venus happens to be "in" the sign of Taurus; otherwise it is false. But the facts of planetary positions constitute a rather unusual set of contingently true facts.

Firstly, they are facts about a limited, interrelated, self-contained, and self-sufficient set of entities. There are seven "wanderers" (the literal meaning of the Greek *planêtai*) visible to the naked eye, neither more nor less. They appear to move in ways peculiar to themselves – but collectively so, not individually; and while one could speculate on a common external cause of their idiosyncratic motions, until Newton's discovery of the principle and laws of gravitation their revolutions remained autonomous and autarkic.

Secondly, whatever the cause and however erratically, the planets nevertheless move with sufficient regularity that ancient astronomers, with the aid of observation and records, were able to construct formulas and models from which they could predict *future* facts. They could say for example not merely that Venus "is now" in Taurus but also on what dates she "will again be" in Taurus. Moreover, if observations were not actually on record – they seldom were – they could also say where she had been on any given date in the past. The construction of the formulas and models which enabled astronomers and astrologers to effect these predictions represents the first solid achievement of "science" as we would define it today.

3 Who Was Where When? Reconstructing Planetary Positions

How in practice did ancient astrologers reconstruct the positions of the planets on their clients' birth dates? Remember that data were not assembled ad hoc at the time of birth; rather, they were calculated for adult clients, mostly some twenty or thirty years afterwards (Jones 1994: 31).

Strangely, the fantasy image of the astrologer scanning the heavens at the very moment of birth persisted in antiquity, a tribute to the hardiness of "urban myths" then as now. Sextus Empiricus, an otherwise hard-headed critic of astrology, has a nice example:

> For by night, they say, the Chaldean [i.e. the astrologer] sat on a high peak watching the stars, while another man sat beside the woman in labour till she should be delivered, and when she had been delivered he signified the fact immediately to the man on the peak by means of a gong; and he, when he heard it, noted the rising Sign [i.e. the sign of the zodiac then rising above the eastern horizon (on which see below)] as that of the horoscope. But during the day he studied the horologes [i.e. sun-dials] and the motions of the sun. (*Adversus mathematicos* 5.27–28, trans. Bury)

The texts and tables that working astrologers did in fact use are now known to us in considerable detail, due largely to Alexander Jones's publication (1999a) of the astronomical papyri from Oxyrhynchus in Egypt. Of these papyrus texts those which are not actual horoscopes appear to have a single common function, to enable astrologers to construct horoscopes.[3] This is most obvious in the class of texts known as "sign-entry almanacs."[4] These almanacs display in three columns, year after year and planet by planet, (a) the month, (b) the day of the month, and (c) the sign entered by the planet on that date. To establish the key data of planetary longitudes (which planets in which signs) all the astrologer had to do was to find the appropriate line for his client's date of birth in each of seven columns. These data had also been furnished in the earlier Babylonian "almanacs" (Rochberg 1998: 8–9). Again we see a continuity from Babylonian to Greek astrology.

4 Factoring in Daily Revolution; Time and Place of Birth; The *horoscopos* (Ascendant) and Other "Centers"

To say, as I did at the start of section 2, that the positions of the planets in the signs are the "primary data" of astrology is not quite accurate.

There is another datum of equal importance: the sign – strictly, the degree of the sign – which happens to be rising in the east at the time of birth. The rising sign or degree is known as the "ascendant"; the Greek term was *horoscopos* (literally "hour-watcher"), the word which gives us English "horoscope."

The inclusion of the ascendant in a horoscope has important implications. First, it *localizes* the horoscope. *Place* makes a difference, not merely *time*. When the Sun rises for you in (say) Oxford, it is still several hours short of rising for me in Toronto. Yet when it does rise in Toronto, its position in the zodiac will have changed barely a quarter of a degree. From an astrological perspective it makes good sense to include the ascendant and by implication all the other points above and below the horizon through which all celestial bodies appear to wheel every twenty-four hours. If angular relationships such as trine (120°) matter, then surely it must also matter from what direction two planets in a particular aspect beam their influence down upon us. Even individually a planet culminating in "midheaven" must surely have a different effect from the same planet twelve hours later at its nadir ("lower midheaven") beneath the earth, even though in terms of motion around the zodiac the planet's change of position may have been insignificant.

Second, by localizing the horoscope, the inclusion of the ascendant *individualizes* the horoscope. Horoscopic astrology, for all its faults, is an egalitarian enterprise. Before the discovery of the Babylonian horoscopes it used to be thought that the individualism implicit in genethlialogy was peculiarly Greek. Nowadays we might rather say that the Greek spirit of *competitive* individualism drove the *development* of the principles of genethlialogy as the rules of a game open to all, to which in fact we are all committed merely by being born. Birth, like death, is a great equalizer.

To return to our metaphorical clock, we must now imagine that while the seven planetary hands turn at different speeds in a counter-clockwise direction (with allowance for occasional retrograde motion for five of them), *the entire dial or clock-face, together with the seven planetary hands, rotates in the opposite direction, clockwise, so rapidly that it completes a rotation in a mere twenty-four hours.* The rotation of the entire dial represents the apparent daily revolution of all celestial bodies without exception, which of course is an epiphenomenon of the actual daily rotation of planet earth under our feet.

Let us now imagine this spinning clock set in a stationary frame. The axle of the spinning clock rests on a frictionless socket on the top edge of a slab with a slot in which the dial can rotate. The top edge of the slab represents the local horizon, which thus bisects the spinning dial into visible and invisible semicircles, the celestial contents of which constantly change as the stars and planets rise and set.

If an observer in the northern (terrestrial) hemisphere faces south and then looks east to her left, she will see the celestial bodies and the signs of the zodiac rising one after another in the east. The equivalent of the rising point on our horoscopic clock is nine o'clock on the stationary frame. The ascendant, then, is whatever sign or degree happens to reach that point at the moment of birth. To the right on the other side (at three o'clock) is the setting point in the west: whatever sign or degree occupies it is the "descendant." Above at the zenith of the frame (twelve o'clock) is "midheaven" and below at the nadir (six o'clock) "lower midheaven." The scheme of the four "centers," as they were called is displayed in figure 3.2.[5]

To cast a horoscope one stops the clock, as it were, and reads off the positions. Note that one can determine not just the sign or degree at each of the four centers but also the positions of each of the planets relative to the centers. The position of the Sun can be determined directly from the time of day, and vice versa. If it was midday, then by definition the Sun was at midheaven; if it was midnight, the Sun was at lower midheaven.

5 A Complication: Consequences of the Obliquity of the Ecliptic

Basic Greek horoscopes identify only the ascendant. From the ascendant one can readily identify the descendant: simply add (or subtract) 180°. However, if you were to assume that midheaven can be identified by

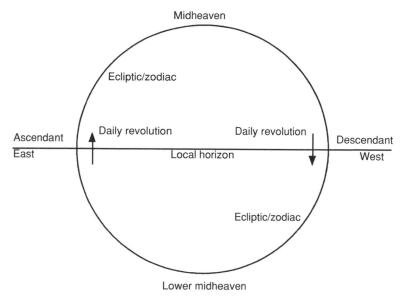

Figure 3.2 The four "centers"

subtracting 90° from the ascendant and lower midheaven by adding 90°, you would be mistaken. Sometimes the angular distance between the ascendant and midheaven is less than 90° and sometimes it is greater; likewise the distance between the ascendant and lower midheaven. There is however a strict condition on this variance: the amount by which the distance between the ascendant and midheaven is less than 90° is always the same as the amount by which the distance between the ascendant and the lower midheaven is greater than 90°, and so on. In other words, the line connecting midheaven and lower midheaven through the clock's center is always a straight line. Thus from the midheaven you can always deduce the lower midheaven: as with the ascendant and descendant simply add (or subtract) 180°. Deluxe horoscopes frequently supply the longitudes of both ascendant and midheaven, as do those embedded in the literary texts.

What causes this apparent paradox? The short answer is the obliquity of the ecliptic. To explain, the band of the zodiac and its median line, the ecliptic, are not parallel to the circles which carry all celestial bodies in their apparent daily orbits around the earth. We can comprehend this fact simply by recalling the annual and daily travels of the Sun. At the height of summer the Sun rises in the north-east, culminates high in the south at midday and sets in the north-west; conversely, in the depths of winter he rises in the south-east, culminates low in the sky to the south at midday, and sets in the south-west. This happens because all the time the Sun is repeating his daily westward circuits he is also moving slowly around the ecliptic along an annual route which takes him not only eastward but also *southward* from the summer solstice to the winter solstice and back again *northward* from the winter solstice to the summer solstice. The ecliptic, then, is *oblique* to the celestial equator, parallel to which all celestial bodies perform their daily circuits. The angle of this obliquity is about 23½°.

Setting aside the actual position of the Sun, let us now imagine a situation in which the northernmost point on the ecliptic, the summer solstice, is the ascendant. This point, as we have seen, will be rising not merely on the eastern horizon but specifically in the north-east. Simultaneously, the winter solstice, as the descendant, will be setting in the south-west. But the midheaven by definition is the point of culmination, which is always due south on the meridian. It follows then that the arc of the ecliptic from the ascendant to midheaven will be longer than the arc from midheaven to the descendant. Twelve hours later, when the point of the summer solstice has completed half a revolution and is now the descendant, the situation is reversed: the arc of the ecliptic from the winter solstice, which is now the ascendant, to midheaven is shorter than the arc from midheaven to the descendant. The only time when the two arcs are precisely equal is when the equinoctial points are the ascendant and the descendant. As with any other pair of opposite points on the ecliptic this happens twice a day.

Since this is a *brief* history of ancient astrology, I do not want to linger over this complication – and be assured, it is the most complicated piece of celestial kinematics I shall inflict on you. Nevertheless, it cannot be ignored. It is an important factor in genethlialogy at any level above the most basic, and in discussing it we can appreciate how Greek astrology was an expression – a regrettable expression, if you will – of the astronomy of its times. Astrology's error lay more in its false assumptions about celestial cause and terrestrial effect than in any failure to comprehend or manipulate the basic positional astronomy required.

Our metaphor of the horoscopic clock descended into paradox precisely because it did not factor in the obliquity of the ecliptic. To accommodate this factor we must suppose that the clock-face or dial, which represents the plane of the ecliptic, is actually mounted askew on its axis of rotation like a wobbling wheel. Consequently, as the dial turns, one half of the rim will always be closer to the clock's reader than the other half. The closest point on the rim represents the summer solstice at the extreme north of the ecliptic, the furthest point the winter solstice at the southern extreme.

In order to represent a horoscope on piece of paper, you must compensate for the loss of the third dimension (depth of the clock from front to back) by imagining that the markers for midheaven and lower midheaven at the top and bottom of the frame oscillate in tandem. When the summer solstice is the ascendant, the midheaven and lower midheaven reach the furthest points of their clockwise swing; and when the winter solstice is the ascendant, they reach the furthest points of their counter-clockwise swing. When the equinoxes are the ascendant and descendant, midheaven and lower midheaven are at the mid-point of their oscillation at twelve and six o'clock respectively (see the three diagrams in figure 3.3).

How large is the oscillation? It all depends on the terrestrial latitude of the horoscope; in other words, on how far north – or in principle south – of the earth's equator the native is born. The further north, the greater the oscillation. So every horoscope is geographically latitude-specific as well as longitude-specific.

To express terrestrial latitude Greek astronomers and geographers did not use the degree scale from zero at the equator to ninety at the pole as we do (and as they did for ecliptic-based celestial latitude). Instead they employed a scale of numbered and named "climates" (Greek *klimata*), typically seven in all, which were *zones* rather than lines of latitude.[6] For

(a) Cancer rising, Capricorn setting

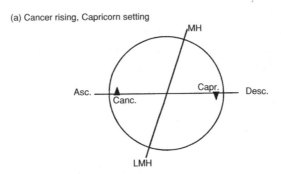

(b) Capricorn rising, Cancer setting

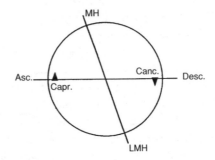

(c) Aries rising, Libra setting (MH and LMH are in the same positions when Libra rises and Aries sets)

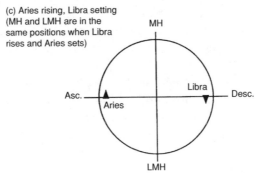

Figure 3.3   Oscillation of midheaven and lower midheaven

each zone the length of the longest day was calculated (to the nearest half-hour), in other words the time interval between sunrise and sunset on the day of the summer solstice. For example, the third climate north from the equator, which is the climate of Lower Egypt, has a maximum of fourteen hours of daylight, while the fourth, the climate of Rhodes, has a maximum of fourteen and a half.

6 Science and the Horoscope

This completes our survey of the astronomical data needed to construct a horoscope in the ancient world and of the geometrical model of heaven and earth which furnished the matrix for the data. Since the data are appearances only, in other words the *apparent* positions of the celestial bodies relative to a particular terrestrial locality, the advances of science have not significantly changed them or affected their limited validity. Astrology never was and never claimed to be astrophysics. The only new *facts* of which modern astrologers are obliged to take cognizance are the positions of the trans-Saturnian planets, Uranus, Neptune, and Pluto, unknown to their colleagues two millennia ago.

A standard Greek horoscope in itself is not a very impressive document, just a list of planetary positions and the sign of the zodiac which happened to be rising locally on someone's date of birth. Its implications however are enormous, for it is a product of a conceptual scheme and a method which, at least in principle, enabled anyone capable of mastering the system to replicate the position of the heavenly bodies from the perspective of any location on the earth's surface not just "now" but well into the past and into the future.

What we would recognize as scientific *knowledge* of celestial phenomena and their behavior was limited to a tiny class of astronomers, mathematicians, philosophers, and the highly educated elite – and to only a minority in the latter two categories. Nevertheless, among the population at large, the "vulgar" as opposed to the "learned," the widespread production of basic horoscopes indicates the first glimmerings of a realistic sense of our actual cosmic environment on earth and in the cosmos. I say "first glimmerings" because it is entirely possible to be a consumer of astrology's products and to remain ignorant of the sphericity of the earth which the system actually postulates.

7 An Example of a Simple Ancient Horoscope – and How to Replicate it with an Astronomical Program on a Home Computer

To conclude this chapter, let us look at an example of an actual horoscope from antiquity. I have selected a relatively early specimen from Neugebauer and Van Hoesen's collection (hereafter N&VH), No. −3.[7] In its simple presentation of the data No. −3 is typical of original horoscopes.[8] However, it does have one unusual feature. After presenting the astronomical data, it issues a warning: "There are dangers. Take care for 40 days because of Mars." We shall return to advice and predictions for the future in a later chapter. They are part – the most important part from a client's point of view – of the meaning and significance imputed to horoscopal data.

Below is the rest of our horoscope (trans. N&VH, with some changes to punctuation and capitalization). Square brackets indicate missing portions of the papyrus. The reconstruction of the lost bits might seem impossibly speculative, until one remembers that the explicit date and time of day, as well as the preserved planetary data and the mention of Aquarius at the lower midheaven, allow a historian of astronomy to reconstruct the missing information with a high degree of probability. The date of the horoscope translates to October 2, 4 BCE, and the time to approximately 9:00 a.m. The planets are listed in the usual order for horoscopes, starting with the two luminaries (Sun and Moon) and continuing through the other five in the order of their (presumed) distance from the earth.

> Year 27 of Caesar (Augustus), Phaophi 5 according to the Augustan calendar, about the 3rd hour of the day. Sun in Libra, Moon in Pisces,

Saturn in Taurus, Jupiter in Cancer, Mars in Virgo, [Venus in Scorpio, Mercury in Virgo (?).[9] Scorpio is rising, Leo is at midheaven, Taurus is then] setting, lower midheaven Aquarius.

Any horoscope – to be precise, the astronomical elements of any horoscope – can be replicated on a home computer by using an astronomical program of the sort designed for amateur star-gazers rather than professional historians of astronomy.[10] A horoscope is essentially a snap-shot of the heavens as seen from a particular point on the earth's surface at a particular time on a particular date, and the modern computer and its software allow one to generate at home these views which not that long ago required a visit to a planetarium. The planetarium view is more impressive because of scale and more realistic because it is projected onto a concave hemisphere, but no essential feature of a horoscope is necessarily excluded from the flat computer screen running the astronomical program.

In one respect the computer monitor is superior to the planetarium dome. A horoscope is an *ideal* snap-shot of the heavens, a view which no human eye or camera could ever scan, for it encompasses the half of the zodiac and the semicircle of the places *below* the horizon as well as those above. Capturing the entire horoscope requires a 360° field of view, which in turn necessitates cutting the zodiac, as it were, and displaying it so that one end appears on one side of the replicating surface and the other on the other, as in the familiar two-dimensional map of the entire earth.[11] This I have done in figure 3.4, which replicates N&VH No. −3 in that it is an accurate horoscopic snap-shot as "seen" from Alexandria in Egypt at 9:00 a.m. on October 2, 4 BCE.[12]

A "snap-shot"? Well, hardly – and only if the quotes round "seen" are given due weight. It is the "mind's eye" that "sees" the heavens, and the mind is that of the ancient astrologer suppressing all that is irrelevant to his intent (notably the fixed stars) and supplying what is germane but invisible, notably the ecliptic and the twelve signs.[13] Furthermore, our astrologer is as "ideal" as the snap-shot. In all likelihood, no quasi-visual mental representation underpinned his data, as it would have in the case of antiquity's great geometrical astronomers. Even if it did,

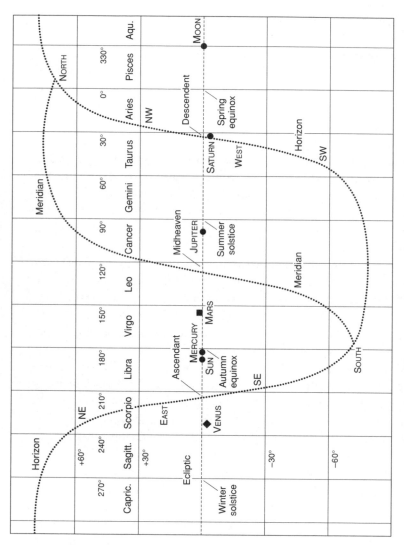

Figure 3.4 The astronomical elements of horoscope N&VH no. −3

the mental model would have been three-dimensional, while what is before your eyes (but not necessarily before your mind's eye) is two-dimensional. Hence the unnatural appearance of the horizon and the meridian.

Here, to conclude, are the horoscope's astronomical data as generated by the computer program for the place, date, and time in question.[14] As you will see, the data are the same as in the papyrus horoscope though more precise.

Sun in Libra 7°, Moon in Pisces 0°, Saturn in Taurus 1°, Jupiter in Cancer 8°, Mars in Virgo 4°, [Venus in Scorpio 21°, Mercury in Libra 1°.[15] Scorpio (3° 30 mins.) is rising, Leo (7°) is at midheaven, Taurus (3° 30 mins.) is then] setting, lower midheaven Aquarius (7° – not displayed in figure).[16]

4

Structure and Meaning in the Horoscope, 1: The Aspects and the "Places"

1 Genethlialogy as a Language; Its Rules of Signification

So your astrologer tells you, for a fee, the positions of the planets and the ascendant at your birth and writes them down on a scrap of paper. What then follows? No predictions accompany the basic standard horoscopes which archaeologists and papyrologists have recovered, so perhaps you ask the astrologer to interpret it for you verbally (for a further fee?). Or perhaps some time later you take it to your astrologer, the same or another, and ask: what does this mean for me now?

In any event, to ask what something means implies that you and your astrologer agree that the configurations of a horoscope mean *something*, just as clouds (frequently) mean rain and smoke (usually) means fire. Actually, it would be better to use the word "signify," for there are obvious causal connections between clouds and rain and between smoke and fire which are not as readily apparent in the case of the things on earth and the things in the heavens. But you and your astrologer at least agree that the stars in their courses *signify* something, whether or not they actually cause it.

To determine what your horoscope *indicates* (another appropriate word), the astrologer does not just make an inspired guess; rather, he refers the elements of your horoscope to a semiotic system of relationships and meanings which in principle is both stable and public. By stable I mean that the relationships and meanings are not subject to random or arbitrary change; by public I mean that the relationships and meanings are in the public domain. No shifting the goal-posts, especially not by the astrologers at dead of night. I describe of course an ideal of stability and public accessibility; in practice, as we shall see, the reality on the ground was quite different.

My point here is one of form, not substance. The question is not whether astrology as a matter of fact succeeds or fails in its predictions, for along with most moderns I take it that astrology generally fails and that its occasional successes are matters of mere coincidence. Rather, my concern is with horoscopic astrology as a system of signs, a language of sorts with its grammar and semantics. That indeed was precisely how St. Augustine at the turn of the fourth and fifth centuries treated it – as a language convention (*On Christian Doctrine* 2.21.32.78–24.37.95). He worried not so much about what it meant as about the demonic speakers with whom one was ineluctably drawn into conversation merely by speaking it. But more of this in a later chapter. In the present chapter we are going to start looking at the structure and semantics of the language of genethlialogy, the rules by which meaning was generated from the astronomical configurations of a horoscope. And rules they are, not facts or pseudo-facts.

Where do we find these rules? In the astrological handbooks, of which a number survive, transmitted copy to copy in manuscript form. They date from the early first century CE to the late fifth. We shall look at them as a class of technical literature in a later chapter. Here they serve simply as the quarry for our source material.

It would be well-nigh impossible to include what every source has to say about every feature of the horoscope's structure and signification. Furthermore, it would be pointless to do so. Within practical limits, it has been done already, more than a century ago by A. Bouché-Leclercq in his heroic *L'astrologie grecque* (1899, reprinted 1963). (If you doubt my epithet, dip into it and see.) Accordingly, I shall select ad hoc different sources to illustrate genethlialogy's various structural features and systems of signification, privileging no particular school and no particular master. For in truth neither a particular school nor a particular master predominated. What I hope to represent is the basic ancient consensus on the main rules of genethlialogy.

Since we are treating genethlialogy as a language, there are two general questions we need to bear in mind. Firstly, is it a *coherent* language, or does it mire its users in contradictions and illogicalities? In sum, is it comprehensible, or is it nonsensical even on its own terms? Secondly, is it an *effective* language? Does it let me efficiently say what I mean?

Let me give an example. Suppose that as your astrologer I have determined that when you were born Mercury was in Virgo and Virgo was at that moment below the eastern horizon and due to start rising in an hour or so. You are a businessman. I then tell you that you have made a smart career choice and your prospects are excellent. Why? Because the system tells me (1) that Mercury is associated with commerce, (2) that Virgo is both the "house" and the "exaltation" of Mercury, and (3) that Mercury, in terms of daily revolution, was then in the second "place," the place of "gain" (*lucrum*). Our general questions, then, are – first, does the system as a whole enable me to generate answer after answer like this one on the same general grounds but for different configurations, and, second, does the system enable me to do so expeditiously?

2 Good and Bad Aspects

At this stage we begin to take into account imputed *value*. What signifies something good, and what signifies something bad? Since the celestial bodies signify not only by their individual selves but also and more fundamentally through their spatial relationships, let us start with the aspects. Which aspects are favorable and which unfavorable?[1] The answer is straightforward – at least as straightforward as anything involving value ever can be. Normally, opposition and quadrature are negative, unfavorable aspects, trine and sextile are positive, favorable aspects. The complications begin when you ask "why?"

To that further question I can return two answers. The first is a blunt "because those are entailments of the aspect signs in the language of astrology." My answer, in other words, is that it's simply a matter of semantics: astrologers have agreed to endow two of these geometrical relationships with negative implications and two with positive implications. Accordingly, in an interpretation an astrologer can confidently assume negative implications for bodies in opposition or quartile aspects to each other and positive implications for bodies in trine or sextile aspects to each other. There may be special circumstances or overriding factors to moderate, cancel out, or even to reverse the normative meanings, but the meanings themselves do not change.

My second answer would address the reasons why astrologers might have agreed to treat one pair of aspects as favorable, the other as unfavorable. In other words, what is the source of this language convention, or is it purely arbitrary? It is here that the real difficulties start, for there is nothing in nature or in our immediate experience to which an astrologer can point so as to suggest that "trine" is in any way good for human beings and "quartile" bad. Put another way, an astrologer cannot justify the values of the aspects in the same way that a chemist or physicist can justify the ordering of the elements in the periodic table. The "reasons" I can find for the values of the aspects will be altogether of another sort. In fact they will not be real reasons at all, but rather rationales which work mostly by manipulating association and analogy. For example, the distinction between good and bad aspects, I suggest, is part of a much wider and more profound system of polarities in Greek thought in which numerical "odd" is on the superior side of the ledger (along with right, straight, light, male, and other "good" properties) and "even" on the inferior side (along with left, curved, dark, female, and other "bad" properties).[2] Trine relates three points and a triangle has three sides, sextile connects two-times-three points and a hexagon has two-times-three sides: "odd" predominates. Quartile relates four points and a square has four sides, a diameter is a line connecting two opposed points: "even" predominates. Ergo trine and sextile good, opposition and quartile bad. Though you may not care for my "explanation," I doubt if you will find Ptolemy's (*Tetr.* 1.13) any more satisfactory: he offers you a choice between harmonics and combinations of signs of the same or of different gender.

Implicit and explicit answers to these sorts of "why" questions can tell us much about the mind-set and world construction of ancient astrology. But they can never *justify* the meanings attributed to its terms and relations. In the end all that can be said is that the meanings are so and not otherwise simply because astrologers have agreed that they are so and not otherwise.

3 Getting a Life: The Twelve "Places"

Next we should look at a new geometrical construct, the division of the circle of the four centers (see chapter 3, section 4) into twelve "places."[3] The circle of the centers thereby becomes the *dôdekatropos* (from the Greek for "twelve" and "to turn" – though actually it is the circle of the zodiac which turns, while the *dôdekatropos* is the fixed circle which frames the turning zodiac) or, more simply, the *dôdekatopos*, the circle of "twelve places."

The places are essential to genethlialogy because they let the astrologer resolve a person's life into its component parts, for example your marriage(s), your health, your material gains. In modern astrology the places are called "houses," but since that term had its own very different meaning in ancient astrology we should stick with "places."

The places are numbered counter-clockwise from the ascendant (see figure 4.1). In other words, the first place runs from the rising point in the east back below the horizon for 30° (from 9 o'clock back to 8 o'clock as it were).[4] Strictly speaking, the lengths of the places vary over the course of a day, expanding and contracting as the midheaven and lower midheaven oscillate to and fro (see above, chapter 3, section 5 with

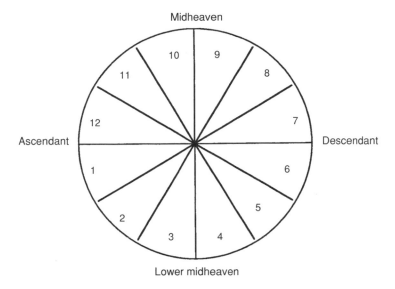

Figure 4.1 The circle of the twelve places

figure 3.3). However, in practice the places were usually treated as equal 30° arcs measured back from the ascendant.

Although each place acquired its own individual name, they were also identified by reference to the centers. Thus, the first, fourth, seventh, and tenth places could themselves be called the ascendant, the lower midheaven, the descendant, and the midheaven. The four places counter-clockwise from each of the cardinal places, namely the second, fifth, eighth, and eleventh places were termed *epanaphorai*, and the four places clockwise, namely the third, sixth, ninth, and twelfth, were termed *apoklimata*. The terms derive from the fact that celestial bodies in the second place will be the "next to rise" after those already in the ascendant, while those in the twelfth place are already "moving [literally "sloping"] away" from the ascendant; and likewise with the places on either side of the other three cardinal places.

Although for the most part theoretical astrologers analyzed the human life into the same set of twelve components and assigned those components to the places in the same sequence, the system was never completely standardized. As an example I have selected the scheme of Hermes Trismegistus, Thrasyllus, and Antiochus of Athens. These are all relatively early, inter-dependent sources, summaries of whose teachings are preserved in manuscripts still extant. I translate below a passage from one of these manuscripts as transcribed in *CCAG* 8.3.116.32–117.27.[5]

> He [Antiochus] next describes the twelve places of the horoscope and their names and significances – thus: that [no. 1] the ascendant is the steering oar of the life and the entry into living, and that it is indicative of the soul and the character and so on; that [2] its *epanaphora* is the place of hopes and what corresponds to them; that [3] the third place from the ascendant is called the place of the Goddess and is indicative of friends and suchlike; and he says that [4] the fourth place, which is the place of lower midheaven [Greek *hypogeion* = "underground"], is called the home and the hearth and is indicative of material possessions, good birth, landed property, and suchlike; that [5] the fifth place from the ascendant is called Good Fortune and signifies living property [i.e. slaves as well as what we call "livestock"] and increase of livelihood; that [6] the sixth place is called Daemon and *prodysis* ["(place) before the descendant"] and is indicative of troubles, sufferings, and enemies; that [7] the seventh, the descendant, is indicative of the last age and end of life; that [8] the eighth is called the *epikatadysis* ["(place of) next setting"] and the futile sign; that [9] the ninth is called the place of the God or the *apoklima* of the midheaven and is indicative of travel and living abroad; that [10] the tenth, which is also the midheaven, is the summit of life and concerns reputation, activity, and professional skills; also the middle span of life and everyday fortune; that [11] the eleventh is called the *epanaphora* of the midheaven and the Good Daemon and signifies future growth; that [12] the twelfth is called the *apoklima* and the Daemon and Necessity and signifies difficulties and problems after conception. Some say it foretells conception.

The passage continues with a brief description of an alternative scheme, the *oktatopos* (sic), a circle of "eight places" rather than twelve.

[Antiochus says] that some made use of the so-called *oktatopos* for the same inquiry. The ascendant [no. 1, 9–7:30 o'clock] they called the place of life; for from it matters of life itself are considered. The *epanaphora* of the ascendant [2, 7:30–6] discloses the things that attend a life. The third place [6–4:30] they called that of brothers, the fourth [4:30–3] that of parents, the fifth [3–1:30] that of children, the sixth [1:30–12] that of bodily defects, the seventh [12–10:30] the place of marriage, and the eighth [10:30–9] that of the end. Through these eight places they examine the whole life of the native.

The *oktatopos* is certainly the simpler and more straightforward of the two schemes. It may be that it was also the earlier and gave ground to the *dôdekatropos* because the latter, with its match of twelve places and twelve signs of the zodiac, seemed intuitively more appropriate.

Since no single source or cluster of sources furnishes either a definitive nomenclature or a definitive classification of the components of a human life, it would be best to complement the passages above with a simple list of the principal life components for each place, together with the names (other than those which merely reflect these components) of the places – see table 4.1.

There is more to the system of places than the mere distribution of a life's experience into its component parts. First the places are related to each other by aspect; and aspect, in particular aspect to the first place (qua ascendant), determines relative importance and power. In addition, all four cardinal places (nos. 1, 4, 7, 10) are important and powerful in and of themselves. (The fact that they are in quartile aspect to each other has to be overlooked, since otherwise the sinister implications of quadrature would vitiate the entire system.) Second, some of the places have an independent bias towards good luck, others towards bad luck. This is self-evidently the case with Good Fortune and Bad Fortune (Places 5 and 6) and with Good Daemon and Bad Daemon (Places 11 and 12).[6]

Since power flows from the ascendant, we find it not only in the other three cardinal places but also in those places in trine and sextile aspects to the first place. This raises the importance of the third, fifth, ninth,

Table 4.1 The fixed circle of the twelve astrological "places"

Place no.	Component of life and alternative name
1	Life (in its entirety)
2	Gain (material prosperity); Gate of the Underworld
3	Brothers (siblings and relatives other than parents and children); Goddess (i.e. the Moon)
4	Parents (and patrimony)
5	Children; Good Fortune
6	Illness; Bad Fortune
7	Marriage
8	Death
9	Travel (and living abroad); God (i.e. the Sun)
10	Honors (and activities)
11	Friends; Good Daemon
12	Enemies; Bad Daemon

and eleventh places, and it leaves the second, sixth, eighth, and twelfth places as relatively unimportant. Hence Antiochus' characterization of the eighth place as "futile" in the passage quoted above. Here is what another early Greek astrologer, Dorotheus of Sidon (mid-first century CE), has to say about the ordering of the places in both importance and desirability:[7]

> The following are the good places in their order of importance: the first is the ascendant [place no. 1], the second the midheaven [no. 10], the third the Good Daemon [no. 11], the fourth Good Fortune [no. 5]; after these, the descendant [no. 7], then the lower midheaven [no. 4], and last of all the ninth place [no. 9] called God. Those are the good places. The bad places are the second [no. 2], the third from the ascendant [no. 3], and the eighth [no. 8]. The remaining two places, the sixth [no. 6] and the twelfth [no. 12], are the worst.

The circle of the places is the most arbitrary of the major astrological constructs. It is therefore the most in need of an appropriate analogy

46

from the earthly and human world to endow it with the aura of naturalness. One can think of the circle of places not just as the sum of a life's activities, relationships, and types of experience but also as the *course* of a life, having, like a drama, "a beginning, a middle, and an end." But the *dôdekatropos* is a circle, and a circle has neither a beginning nor an end. So on what criteria do we choose one place or another as the first? Surely the proper starting point is the place where celestial bodies *rise to birth* (note how the master metaphor is slipped into place), namely the ascendant. Like the apparent Sun during the course of a day, a human life rises to birth, reaches the high noon of its maturity, then declines towards "sunset" and death. Note that another metaphor is also in play, as it is in virtually every part of genethlialogy: the assimilation of "up," "top," and "ascending" with growth and waxing power, and of "down," "bottom," and "descending" with decrease and waning power.

The metaphor of "rising to birth" (and so on) explains the primacy of the ascendant as the place of "Life" in its entirety. The ascendant dominates the horoscope. "From this place," says Firmicus Maternus, an astrologer of the fourth century CE, "the fundamentals of the entire nativity may be ascertained.... It is the pivot, the fixing, the substance of the entire nativity" (*Mathesis* 2.19.2). As part of the same metaphor, midheaven, the place (no. 10) in which celestial bodies are at or reaching culmination, indicates the summit of a career and the native's accomplishments. It is the place of "Honors," of mature activities, of one's profession and skills. On the west or setting side of the circle we find the place of "Death," not indeed in the descendant itself (no. 7), but in the place occupied by celestial bodies which will be the "next to set" (no. 8, *epicataphora*, Firmicus 2.19.9). Note, however, that in the early system of Hermes, Thrasyllus, and Antiochus, quoted above, the descendant itself is "indicative of the last age and end of life," while the preceding place (no. 6) is just as sinister ("indicative of troubles, sufferings, and enemies"), and the following place (no. 8) is impotent ("futile"). Also, the "Gates of Dis" (= Pluto, lord of the underworld), normally used as an alternative name for the second place ("Gain"), are in fact set where they belong, to the west in the descendant, by the astrological poet Manilius (*Astronomica* 2.948–58) writing early in the first century CE.[8]

The metaphor of a life rising at birth and setting at death can be pressed only so far, for it cannot convincingly accommodate the underground places which, strictly speaking, would have to precede birth and follow death (nos. 2–6). Here a different metaphor or, rather, a different set of associations comes into play. The underground in ancient thought is not only the place of the dead but also the source of new life, especially of vegetation which literally rises from the ground. It is also the source of metals and of wealth generated from the precious metals, gold and silver, as also of buried treasure. Consequently the places deep underground are not at all sinister. On the contrary, the second place is the place of "Gain" (or, in Antiochus' scheme, of the "Hope" of gain), and the fourth place, the lower midheaven (or "underground" in Greek), is the place of property, especially of landed property handed down as patrimony. Wealth and increase come also from the womb, where it is "sown" as seed and "hidden" until it emerges from the dark into the light of day. So the womb is a potent underground, and that is why the underground places are the sites of the human family as it constantly regenerates itself. Appropriately, this is the sector of the circle concerned with children, parents, and siblings, as also with the family's human and animal livestock. We can now also appreciate why the "Gates of Dis," the door to the underworld, are set in the second place, the place of "Gain" (*lucrum* in Latin). In both Greek and Latin the words for rich/riches are virtually the same as the names of the god of the underworld and lord of the dead, Pluto in Greek and Dis in Latin. Wealth comes from the world below.

In sectoring a life and isolating its components those who devised the circle of the places could not help also defining a *normative* life for the culture of their times. Of what does a life consist? That is the question which the scheme implicitly answers – and answers in a manner acceptable to the profession's clients. Even the most cursory look shows that the template of the twelve places implies a person of some substance and status, someone who (as the saying goes) *has* a life, someone above mere subsistence level, someone of more consequence than a slave or peasant restricted to brutal physical labor without respite – which immediately rules out the majority of the population.[9] Yes, this undercuts what I was saying in chapter 3 about astrology's egalitarian implications. It has to be admitted that astrology, at least the sort of astrology found in the handbooks, was not generally for the riff-raff. Similarly, although women's lives can be accommodated to the scheme, the implied or "ideal" native is clearly male. By and large, only men had the sort and degree of agency in their lives that the scheme of the places implies.

Conclusion

Before moving on from the astrological places to the zodiac and its signs, as we shall do in the next chapter, I want to conclude with an analogy to another form of ancient divination, the Roman practice of auspicy, observing bird flight, and augury, listening to the cries of birds. These practices – they are really two parts of the same activity – required the definition of a site in which bird flight and bird calls could be observed and heard. This site, called a "temple" (*templum*), was strictly defined with reference to the official observer (the Augur, that is, or the executive with the right and obligation to take the "auspices"): a left side, a right side, a front, and a back.

This augural definition of a tract of space relative to the observer parallels the astrologer's definition of the circle of the twelve places relative to the horizon at the place of birth. Coincidentally, both practices postulated a south-facing observer (although not always in augury). I am not suggesting that Graeco-Roman astrology consciously drew on Roman augural theory and practice or even that contemporaries were aware of the analogy.[10] Nevertheless the comparison is worthwhile because it reveals similar ways of going about similar practices, in this instance two different modes of divination.

5

Structure and Meaning in the Horoscope, 2: The Zodiac and its Signs

1 Introduction

In chapter 3 we looked at the zodiac as an astronomical construct. We saw that it is a notional band on the celestial sphere extending some 6° on either side (north and south) of the ecliptic. The ecliptic is the annual path of the Sun around the heavens. It is a "great" circle in that it bisects the celestial sphere into two equal hemispheres. By convention and for metrological purposes it starts at the vernal equinox, which is one of the two points where it intersects the celestial equator. The celestial equator is also a great circle – one may think of it as a projection outwards into space of the terrestrial equator – and it too divides the celestial sphere into two equal hemispheres, one to the north and the other to the south. The celestial sphere rotates (in appearance) once a day, its axis of rotation passing not only through the terrestrial poles but also through the celestial poles, those points around which the stars on a clear night appear to revolve. Remember that the zodiac with its twelve signs is also revolving, but because of the obliquity of the ecliptic it turns like a wheel very badly out of alignment (above, chapter 3, section 5).

Diametrically opposite the vernal equinox is the autumn equinox. At the vernal equinox the Sun crosses from south to north of the equator and at the autumn equinox from north to south. The relation of the ecliptic/zodiac to the celestial equator is shown in figure 5.1.

The twelve signs of the zodiac are equal in length, so each of them occupies a sector of 30°. Distance along the ecliptic or celestial "longitude" was expressed in terms of sign plus degree of sign: thus a planet at longitude 45° (from the vernal equinox) would be said to be at Taurus 15°, for Taurus, qua the second sign, spans the sector 30°–60°. As already noted in chapter 3 (section 1), Greek astrologers for some time continued to use older Babylonian schemes which placed the vernal equinox at Aries 8° or 10°, though the Greek – and modern – astronomical norm of Aries 0° eventually prevailed. We shall not concern ourselves here with the Babylonian schemes except when unavoidable. The axis at right angles to celestial longitude is celestial "latitude." Greek genethlialogy is almost exclusively concerned with the longitude of the planets, in other words the sign and degree in which a planet is, was, or will be. Consideration of latitude, in other words how far north or south of the ecliptic a planet happens to be, plays little part. We shall look at some significant exceptions in due course.

In this chapter we shall look at the zodiac and its signs as a self-contained system, postponing to the next chapter consideration of the

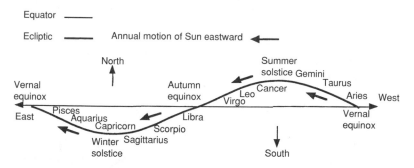

Figure 5.1 The ecliptic, the signs of the zodiac, and the celestial equator

significance of various planets in various signs. In looking at the internal relations of the zodiac, we are looking at things which do not change. Aries is in trine aspect to Leo and will always be so. Taurus is a female sign (yes, female), and that too will not change as long as the convention which alternates gender (odd-numbered signs male, even-numbered female) persists. Such things are not really facts or non-facts (although one could call many of them "factoids"), and there is no way in which they can be confirmed or disconfirmed; rather, they are agreed "truths" in the discourse of astrology.

What does change – and changes quite rapidly – is the position of the zodiac and thus of its twelve signs against the fixed circle of the twelve places. As the signs revolve through the places they acquire and shed in succession the associations and significance of every place. Those meanings, which concern the stages and components of a life, we surveyed in the preceding chapter.

2 Orientation

A comparison with the *dôdekatropos* is a good starting point for an examination of the zodiac, for both are celestial circles divided arbitrarily into twelve sectors. From that initial similarity let us now look at the differences. First and most obviously the zodiac revolves (daily with "universal" motion) while the circle of the twelve places is stationary. However, in another sense the *dôdekatropos* is highly mobile: it migrates from one terrestrial location to another and for each horoscope it is specific to the native's place of birth, while the location of the zodiac on the celestial sphere is fixed forever. This brings us to another difference: while both circles may be called "celestial," only the zodiac is properly so. The zodiac is written, as it were, on the celestial sphere; the *dôdeka-tropos*, by contrast, is written on a local sky – or more precisely its upper half is written on a local sky, its lower half on a sort of mirror image of that local sky underground, the two semicircles being joined at the ascendant on the eastern horizon and the descendant on the western.

These differences carry implications for orientation and direction and for their representation in diagrams. Important differences will become apparent if we compare the diagram of the *dôdekatropos* in figure 3.2 (or 3.3 or 4.1) with the diagram of the zodiac in figure 5.1. The diagram of the *dôdekatropos* represents a view of the sky and the corresponding "underground" *southwards*. Hence the view and the diagram of the view have an east side to the left and a west side to the right (and vice versa for southern hemisphere viewers who will be looking northwards). What, then, of north and south? The logic of both view and diagram puts south in front of the observer and north behind; hence they cannot be represented in the diagram at all, since it lacks the necessary third dimension. In the two dimensions actually viewed the axis at right angles to the east–west axis is an up–down or zenith–nadir axis, not a north–south axis. So far we have been speaking of the four cardinal points and the two axes in the terrestrial sense. When we turn to the zodiac and its representation (figure 5.1) we have to treat the same terms in the celestial sense, since what is observed and represented is a tract of the heavens, in this instance a complete band beginning and ending at the vernal equinox (where we have, as it were, snipped the band in order to display it in two dimensions on the page). The upper half of the diagram, above the celestial equator, represents the northern celestial hemisphere and the lower half the southern celestial hemisphere, so "up" is north and "down" is south. Similarly east is towards the left and west towards the right. Note that I do not speak of an east side and a west side, for east and west are always relative, and no part of the celestial sphere is the east or the west in an absolute sense. The same of course is true of the terrestrial globe. Only in views and representations of *parts* of either sphere can a *side* be termed the east or the west. Celestially, east and west are first and foremost *directions* of motion. The extra-terrestrial universe revolves westward and, from the ancient point of view, "to the right"; the seven planets move eastward and "to the left" (with spells of westward "retrograde" motion for five of them).

3 Signs and Seasons: The Four Primary Quadrants of the Zodiac

That six of the signs of the zodiac are northern and six southern is an astronomical fact, not an astrological convention. Most of the other significant facts about the zodiac and its signs also have to do with the annual journey of the Sun in sequence through them. Figure 5.1 displays this familiar journey, beginning at the vernal equinox at the start of Aries (longitude 0°). From there the Sun climbs northward through Aries, Taurus, and Gemini to the summer solstice at the start of Cancer (90°). From the summer solstice he begins to descend through Cancer, Leo, and Virgo to the autumn equinox at the start of Libra (180°), and thence on down through Libra, Scorpius, and Sagittarius to the winter solstice at the start of Capricorn (270°). Finally, he begins to climb again through Capricorn, Aquarius, and Pisces, and so back to the vernal equinox at the start of Aries (360° = 0°).

Our first division of the zodiac is accordingly into four seasonal quadrants (see figure 3.1 as well as 5.1):

1. Spring – vernal equinox to summer solstice: Aries, Taurus, Gemini.
2. Summer – summer solstice to autumn equinox: Cancer, Leo, Virgo.
3. Autumn – autumn equinox to winter solstice: Libra, Scorpius, Sagittarius.
4. Winter – winter solstice to vernal equinox: Capricorn, Aquarius, Pisces.

Most people now construe the solar journey in temporal rather than spatial terms. Indeed, they do not think of it as a journey at all, but rather as an annual cycle, the cycle of the four seasons with their official starting dates at the equinoxes (spring and autumn) and solstices (summer and winter). Note how the equinoxes from this point of view are considered moments in time rather than points in space. In fact they are both, and the change is merely a shift of emphasis.

For Ptolemy (*Tetr.* 1.10) this division of the zodiac into four seasonal quadrants was primary, since of all the ways of brigading the signs this alone is founded on a demonstrable link between astronomical cause (the Sun's progress around the ecliptic) and climatic effect (seasonal weather patterns). Second to this is the set of three squares formed by the first, second, and third signs in each quadrant: (1) the equinoctial and solstitial signs – Aries, Cancer, Libra, Capricorn; (2) the "solid" signs – Taurus, Leo, Scorpius, Aquarius – so called because they consolidate or firm up (at least in our perception, Ptolemy adds astutely) the seasonal weather initiated by the preceding signs; (3) the bicorporal or double signs – Gemini, Virgo, Sagittarius, Pisces. The third set is the most interesting for those like us wanting to see how ancient astrologers built significance into their system. For Ptolemy the "double" significance of the bicorporal signs lies in the fact that in concluding each season these signs give a foretaste of the weather to come in the next season. But that is not actually why they were *called* "bicorporal." The term itself derives from the fact that there are two Gemini twins, Castor and Pollux, that there are two fishes in Pisces, that Sagittarius is a centaur, part horse and part human, and that Virgo is composed of two elements, the Maiden herself and the stalk and ear of wheat she carries (the star Spica).[1] What are Ptolemy and his colleagues up to here? In a nutshell, they find an entirely new application for the term "double-bodied" and justify its new meaning by appeal to its original intent. The logic goes somewhat as follows. The weather when the Sun is in Pisces is a little like spring even though it's still winter. The celestial emblem of this fact is the two fishes of Pisces. Note that I say "emblem," not "cause," for the latter would be quite unfair – at least to Ptolemy. Astrology does indeed carry an excess of reasons, but they are not necessarily pseudo-causal reasons.

4 Instantiating Contraries: North and South, Up and Down, High and Low, Rising and Falling, Growth and Decay, Success and Failure, Exaltation and Humiliation

Going north, as the Sun does in winter and spring, is metaphorically an ascent and going south a descent. Similarly, the summer or northern solstice is the "high" point of the solar journey and the winter or southern solstice the "low" point. The underlying metaphor is not a recent one. It was current in Greek and Latin and thus in the thinking of Greek-speakers and Latin-speakers. It is what we call a "dead" metaphor, so trite that it scarcely registers as a metaphor at all. Yet for all their lifelessness dead metaphors do much more of the heavy lifting in language and in thought than do their living and lively siblings.

From physical location "above" and "below" and physical motion "up" or "down" the metaphor was extended, then as now, to encompass success and failure in human life, "high" status and "low" status, "upward mobility" and "downward mobility" (in the sanitized expressions of today). It also applies – and was applied to – the cycle of plant life: vegetation "springs up" and "dies down."

The annual up-and-down journey of the Sun, which is actually a journey northwards from the winter solstice to the summer solstice and back again, was both the linchpin of this metaphor and its exemplary case. As the Sun journeys northward, day after day he appears higher and higher in the noontime sky; likewise lower and lower as he journeys south. As he does so, he draws up vegetation from the earth, bringing it to ripeness, and then burns and desiccates it with the heat of summer so that it withers, collapses, and dies. Yet paradoxically this destruction wrought by the Sun is as beneficial as it is inevitable. Desiccation leads to harvest, and harvest to the preservation of human life through the barren months of winter and to next year's life dormant in the sown grain.

As the Sun inscribes his celestial journey on the earth in the waxing and waning of the seasons, so the ancients inscribed the story of a human life on that same annual journey as the god's own biography, from birth and the weakness of the newborn at the winter solstice on December 25, through growth and waxing vigor to a height of strength and power at the summer solstice, and then into decline, senescence, and a sort of death. Speaking of the differences in age of the representation of various gods, the fourth-century (CE) polymath Macrobius said that these all "relate to the Sun, who is made to appear very small at the winter solstice" (*Saturnalia* 1.18.10). "In this form," he continues, "the Egyptians bring him forth from the shrine on the set date to appear like a tiny infant on the shortest day of the year." By the same metaphorical logic, the Calendar of Antiochus of Athens named December 25 the "Sun's birthday," with the notation "light increases."[2] Here the human story and the solar story necessarily diverge. Each of us on earth has but one "go round," the Sun aloft an infinity. The Sun visibly moves in a circle without beginning and without end,[3] while we, "once our brief light has set, must sleep one single night for ever."[4]

The matters we have been discussing in this section belong to astrology's deep structure, the system of cosmological representations supporting and legitimating the categories of genethlialogy. This deep structure is manifest and explicit in the characterization of the four seasonal quadrants of the zodiac in terms of "exaltation" and "humiliation." In the system of Antiochus of Athens we find the zodiac quartered as follows (*CCAG* 7.127–8, cf. 8.3.112–13):[5]

1. Spring quadrant (vernal equinox to summer solstice): "ascending in the north" = "exaltation exalted."
2. Summer quadrant (summer solstice to autumn equinox): "descending in the north" = "exaltation humiliated."
3. Autumn quadrant (autumn equinox to winter solstice): "descending in the south" = "humiliation humiliated."
4. Winter quadrant (winter solstice to vernal equinox): "humiliation exalted."

Thus named and structured the quartered zodiac starkly illuminates an ironic paradox at the heart of the north/high versus south/low distinction. You ascend towards a summit and you descend from it; you descend towards a nadir and you ascend from it. From the height of good fortune there is nowhere to go but down – add a dash of hubris and you enact the classic tragic plot – and from the depths of bad fortune there is nowhere to go but up – if you survive the fall. The Sun in Capricorn enjoys that guarantee of renewal; we do not.

The terms themselves, "exaltation" and "humiliation," are important in astrology, and we shall meet them again in another technical context in the next chapter. Both the Greek and Latin words for "exaltation" (*hypsôma, altitudo*) mean literally "height" (cf. our "altitude"). The Greek word *tapeinôma*, which I have translated "humiliation," refers as often to low social status as to physical lowness. The Latin word is *deiectio* and means "casting down." In astrological contexts it is usually translated in English as "depression," which is unfortunate since that word, as would "dejection" too, carries irrelevant psychological connotations. The "exalted" in antiquity were the powerful, the "humiliated" or "humble" were the powerless. Not until the arrival of Christianity was merit or virtue ever imputed to "humility."

5 Further Meanings of the Seasonal Quartering (Ptolemy, *Tetr.* 1.10)

At the same time as he divides the zodiac and thus the solar year into seasonal quadrants Ptolemy identifies their predominant characteristics: "Spring exceeds in moisture on account of its diffusion after the cold has passed and warmth is setting in; the summer, in heat, because of the nearness of the sun to the zenith; autumn more in dryness, because of the sucking up of the moisture during the hot season just past; and winter exceeds in cold, because the sun is farthest away from the zenith" (*Tetr.* 1.10, trans. Robbins).

These four seasonal characteristics are not Ptolemy's invention. He is merely utilizing the fundamental categories of Greek physics, standardized by Aristotle almost half a millennium earlier. Matter in our mutable sublunary world instantiates in different combinations two pairs of opposite qualities: the hot and the cold, and the dry and the wet. In combination these opposites produce the four terrestrial elements: fire (hot and dry), air (hot and wet), earth (cold and dry), water (cold and wet).[6]

Accordingly, Ptolemy determines on climatological grounds which pole of which polarity predominates in which season and thus in which quadrant of the zodiac. At the same time he applies the same two pairs of contrary qualities to the stages of the life cycle which he divides into four and associates each with the predominant seasonal quality: the first stage with the moisture of spring, the second with the heat of summer, the third with the dryness of autumn, and the fourth with the cold of winter. He also ties in the four quarters of the earth and the winds which blow from those directions. This is not as straightforward as it might appear. Yes, we can link the hot winds of summer to the south and the cold wind of winter to the north, but we have to suppress, as Ptolemy does, the inconvenient fact that that in summer the Sun is in the *north* celestial hemisphere while in winter he is in the *south*. Furthermore, while one can postulate a dry east wind and a moist west one, no quadrant of the zodiac, as we noted above, is intrinsically either "eastern" or "western." Typically, astrological structures of this sort finally build themselves into self-contradiction and absurdity. There is such a thing as *too much* meaning.

6 Other Ways of Dividing the Zodiac and Grouping the Signs

As we move from the seasonal quartering to other divisions of the zodiac and groupings of the signs the criteria become ever more formal, more arbitrary, and less connected with empirical reality, although reasons for linkage with our actual world are always proffered – as they have to be if celestial causation or signification is to be maintained. Increasingly, though, metaphor and word play take over.

Instead of dividing the zodiac into sectors, as with the seasonal quadrants, one may relate them by aspects. A sign is in bissextile aspect to the sign which is two signs ahead of it and two signs behind it, in quartile aspect to the signs three ahead and three behind, in trine aspect to the signs four ahead and four behind, and of course in opposition to the sign opposite. To take an arrangement already mentioned (section 3), the three sets of equinoctial/solstitial signs, solid signs, and bicorporal signs exemplify the quartile aspect.

By alternating gender around the zodiac, the fundamental zoological polarity of male and female is accommodated, thus creating two hexagons, one of male signs, the other of female signs. Obviously the lead sign, Aries the Ram, has to be male.[7] Two signs on we find the just as obviously male Gemini, and another two signs on from Gemini the just as obviously male Leo. Less felicitously, the female hexagon must begin with Taurus the Bull, but the glaring contradiction was muted by observing in a coy astrological joke that the eponymous constellation was a *protomê*, a "fore-cut" or front-end-only.

An even more fundamental polarity, pervading the entire cosmos, is that between light and darkness, day and night. This polarity can be structured into the zodiac by alternating signs, as with the gender polarity. No prize for guessing correctly that the male signs are the day signs and the female signs are the night signs. Another solution, less patriarchal, is to assign light and the day to the northern signs (Aries to Virgo) and darkness and night to the southern signs (Libra to Pisces) on the grounds that days are longer than nights when the Sun is in the former and night longer than days when he is in the latter. Yet a third solution alternates pairs of contiguous signs (Pisces and Aries day signs, Taurus and Gemini night signs, and so on). All three schemes are presented by Manilius (*Astronomica* 2.203–22).[8]

Of great importance are the four triangles formed by linking every fourth sign (trine aspect), for these configurations connect triads of signs which instantiate the four elements, and of these four elements are constituted all things which physically exist in the world below the Moon:

1. The triangle of fire (dry, male): Aries, Leo, Sagittarius
2. The triangle of earth (cold, female): Taurus, Virgo, Capricorn
3. The triangle of air (hot, male): Gemini, Libra, Aquarius
4. The triangle of water (wet, female): Cancer, Scorpius, Pisces

Notice how the logic is now driven entirely by geometrical schematization. Yes, in the real world fishes do indeed belong in water, but a scorpion has no business in joining them there, and a water-carrier no business in exchanging water for air. Note also how the schematization puts a celestial imprimatur on the social constructions of gender: men are hot and dry, women cold and wet – that is what the configurations of heaven intend.

As a final example of imposing meaning on the geometrical patterns of the zodiac and its signs, let us return to the seasonal quartering formed, as in figure 3.1, by a vertical diameter linking the solstices and a horizontal diameter linking the equinoxes. Across the equinoctial diameter there is an imbalance of power: signs in the upper semicircle (spring and summer) "command" the signs in the lower semicircle, each of whom "hears" or "obeys" his or her counterpart above. The pairs are formed not by diametrical opposition (for example Taurus does not command Scorpius) but by chords at right angles to the equinoctial diameter (Taurus commands Aquarius). An alternative schematization draws the diameter not from one equinoctial *point* to the other but from one equinoctial *sign* to the other. In this scheme Taurus commands Pisces, not Aquarius, and the equinoctial signs neither issue nor receive orders. Shifting to the solstitial (vertical) axis, we find by the same schematization pairs of signs "of equal power" who "look at" each other across the divide. The metaphor changes to sight from imperative speech. The rationale for these two schemes is length of daylight. Signs in which day is longer than night boss around signs in which the opposite pertains; signs with equal daylight eye each other with wary regard.[9] In a variant of the second scheme, discussed in some detail by Firmicus Maternus (*Mathesis* 2.29) along with its Greek pedigree, the signs who "look" at each other project "counter-shadows" (*antiscia*) on each other. These *antiscia* provide additional bases from which the planets can attack or support one another. For example, a planet in Aries can "send an *antiscium*" into, and so operate out of, Virgo; and vice versa. We shall return to the *antiscia* in chapter 7 on the interpretation of horoscopes since Firmicus uses the scheme to explain why an apparently brilliant horoscope led to an actual life with serious set-backs.

7 War in Heaven: Manilius (*Astronomica* 2.466–607) on Friendships and Enmities Between Signs and Groups of Signs

Heaven, like earth, is a place of friendships and enmities, alliances and hostilities. We shall see this most clearly when we come to the planets, which are in fact anthropomorphized gods (or proxies for them) and thus beings who can reasonably be thought to act and feel like humans. But it is worth noticing how the same distinction between friend and foe is imposed on the less tractable material of the signs. How after all does one decide whether a Ram likes or dislikes a pair of Twins, a Lion likes or dislikes a pair of Scales, and an Archer likes or dislikes a Water-carrier? And behind those puzzling questions of the criteria of love and hatred lies the deeper puzzle of why love and hatred should be battling it out in the heavens at all.

To the second question there is an easy, true, and not very interesting general answer: the pioneers of astrology in the ancient world projected the characteristics of humanity and its cultures onto the heavens and then used these projections to explain and justify the way we are as individuals and societies. All the interest, though, lies in the detail. As a case study let us see how Manilius addresses both questions. Manilius was a poet – rather a good one, though that is virtually impossible to convey in translation – which means that his answers to questions of the second sort are imaginative and far from superficial. Imaginative, in a less flattering way, are his answers to questions of the first sort where it is more a matter of ingenuity in versifying mathematical sophistry.

In the middle of a long passage on the friendships and enmities of the signs Manilius (2.466–607, at 520–35) answers our first question: Aries not only dislikes Gemini but also likes Leo and Sagittarius; Leo not only dislikes Virgo but also likes Aries and Sagittarius: Sagittarius not only dislikes Aquarius but also likes Aries and Leo. The likes are easily explained as entailments of the trine aspect in which Aries, Leo, and Sagittarius stand to each other (see above), and the assumption that favorable aspects mean friendly relations. The dislikes spring from the fact that in alternating triangles (nos. 1 and 3, nos. 2 and 4) each of the three signs in one triangle is in opposition to, and therefore also hostile to, one of the signs in the other: Aries to Libra, Leo to Aquarius, Sagittarius to Gemini. From this we may reasonably infer that all members of one of the triangles collectively detest all members of the other triangle. It's all a matter of the properties of a twelve-sector circle, or as Manilius with all the weight and pith of Latin poetry puts it, ... *sic veri per totum consonat ordo* ("thus the design of truth is consistent in every part" (2.522, trans. Goold).

Though the answer is sufficient, Manilius adds another of a different sort – what we might call a "naturalistic" answer based on the signs' own characteristics. One trio is human, the other animal, and "there remains eternal war between men and wild beasts" (2.528). Who prevails? The humans of course, because "reason is greater than brute force" (2.530–1). As usual, there are loose ends to be tied up. A pair of scales is neither human nor animal, but it can be left to common sense to realize that someone has to hold the scales (don't they?) or that scales are a human contrivance (aren't they?). On Sagittarius the Archer Manilius is explicit: Sagittarius is a centaur (isn't he?), so we have to go with the bestial rear-end. Or as he says in an egregious example of his versification at its lamest, "to part of himself the Centaur gives way on account of his rear, to such an extent is manliness restricted to man" (2.533–4). If you find this incomprehensible and awful, do not blame the translator (G. P. Goold) and do not question your own good judgment.

Enmity in Manilius' rather dark and pessimistic world view is much more prevalent than friendship, and some of these celestial enmities, he says, cannot be explained by geometrical relationships alone. "Nevertheless, there are individual signs which follow their own caprice and, having private foes, wage wars of their own. The Ram's children are at war with the offspring of the Virgin, the Balance, and the Twins, and with those whom the Urn [Aquarius] has brought forth. Against the progeny of the Bull there advance men born under the Crab and under the Scales, and those produced by the fierce Scorpion and by the Fishes"

(2.539–45, trans. Goold).[10] These enmities cascade down from heaven on to us earthlings who inherit them according to the signs "under" which we are born.

And what's to be learnt from this celestial mayhem?

> From so many configurations of signs come beings opposed to each other, and thus variously and thus often is enmity created. For this reason nature has never created from herself anything more precious or less common than the bond of true friendship.... And throughout the long history of mankind, ages and centuries so many, amid so many wars and the motley strife even of peace, when misfortune calls for loyal support, it scarce finds it anywhere. There was but one Pylades, but one Orestes, eager to die for his friend [mythological heroes, the archetypes of "buddies in bad times"]. Yet how great is the sum of villainy in every age. How impossible to relieve the earth of its burden of hate. (2.579–82, 589–93, trans. Goold)

Never far from the minds of thinkers and poets in the late first century BCE and early first century CE were the horrors of the death throes of the Roman republic and the civil wars which attended its final collapse and the later struggles for supremacy among the would-be successors of the assassinated Julius Caesar. In the event the last Big Man standing, Augustus, did in fact bring lasting peace and prosperity to the Roman empire, but when Manilius was writing at the end of Augustus' "principate" and the beginning of that of his adopted son Tiberius, fear of renewed anarchy still haunted the consciousness of all thoughtful persons. In the dozen or so lines which follow Manilius shows us vignettes of the old anarchy, its deep hatreds, transitory alliances, and betrayals. And then he draws the lesson: "Truly, *since many are the signs in which men are born for discord,* peace is banished throughout the world, and the bond of loyalty is rare and granted to few; and just as in heaven, so too is earth at war with itself, and the nations of mankind are subject to a destiny of strife" (2.603–7, trans. Goold).

Few of us today would endorse Manilius' model of astral causation. However, the empirical falsity of the model should not over-much concern us. Ancient astrology, I contend, retains value as an *imaginative* structure in which the astronomically/astrologically constructed heavens function as a sort of template imposed on terrestrial and human affairs in order to discern structure and meaning in the here and now. Writing this chapter in July 2005, I do not think I have to make the case for Manilius' "relevance."

As a bitter-sweet coda, Manilius does discern one truly nice guy among the signs, Aries the Ram. Yet his very niceness exposes him to betrayal by his trigonal colleagues, Leo and Sagittarius. "Yet the Ram is a simple creature and shows more respect for the children of the Lion and the Centaur's [Sagittarius'] progeny than they for him. He is by nature a gentle sign, exposed to the harm that falls on gentleness; he is devoid of deceit, and his heart is as soft as his fleecy body. His fellow signs are marked by ferocity and a lust for spoil, and their covetous spirit oft impels them to break faith for their own ends; and their gratitude for a kindness is short-lived" (2.611–18, trans. Goold).

If I have spent rather a long time on the friendships and enmities of signs, it is to give a sample of what I find of abiding value in ancient astrology and an answer – there are others – to the question I shall pose in chapter 9: why bother with it today?

8 The Individual Signs; The Signs and Human Occupations

The individual character of a sign and its particular sphere of influence are determined not only by its position in the seasonal cycle and other sequences (male/female, fiery/earthy/airy/watery, and so on) but also by the qualities, real or imagined, of the terrestrial referents of the underlying constellations.[11] This sounds complicated but is actually quite simple, as a single example will show. The sign of Leo (longitude 120°–150°) is so named from the constellation Leo with which in antiquity it more or less coincided. Leo, like several other zodiacal constellations and signs, had his origins in Babylon whence he was imported into Greek astronomy and astrology. If signs have characters and if they influence those born "under" them in certain ways related to their characters,[12] it follows that Leo is fierce and predatory and those born under him will exhibit the same character traits (which as rational moral agents they have both the ability and the obligation to control).

Animals have always stalked emblematically down trails of metaphorical association. Lions are not only fierce and predatory, they are also "brave" and "regal." In antiquity (as also in "primitive" cultures surviving into modern times) these imputed qualities were more numerous and more subtly articulated than now. To many a Greek or Roman, lions were as truly "fiery" as they were "fierce," and if that is unsurprising, note that they were also sexually austere – lions, that is, not lionesses – and rational moral agents: man-eaters, if caught, were liable to human criminal punishment, crucifixion; on the side of law and order and as agents of the gods' anger, they would appear to perjurers in their dreams.[13] Astrology, accordingly, could bring to bear a rich array of associations, much of it not immediately obvious to us today, and so endow the signs with correspondingly rich characters and portfolios of influence on human affairs. Of course some signs had more potential than others: just how much metaphorical freight can a Crab or a pair of Fishes or a pair of Scales carry?

Early in the fourth book of his *Astronomica* (4.122–293) Manilius surveys "the characters, the predominant quality, the pursuits, and the different skills which the signs impart" (4.122–3, trans. Goold). As one of the more straightforward matches of emblem to character and occupation (which is what he means by "pursuits" and "skills"), here is what he has to say about Pisces the Fishes: "The folk engendered by the two Fishes ... will possess a love of the sea; they will entrust their lives to the deep, will provide ships or gear for ships and everything that the sea requires for activity connected with it" (4.273–6, trans. Goold). So in addition to the shipwrights and ships' chandlers Manilius mentions navigators, fishermen (naturally), and the navy. Characteristically, "the children of this sign are endowed with fertile offspring [if this were true, natural selection would have put us all under Pisces aeons ago!], a friendly disposition, swiftness of movement, and lives in which everything is ever apt to change" (4.290–1, trans. Goold).

The children of Pisces must share the element of water with Aquarians. Professionally, Manilian Aquarians (4.259–72) are hydrologists and hydraulic engineers. They are dowsers (water-diviners); they design water-driven mechanisms; they engineer artificial lakes and canals; they build coastal villas on man-made promontories;[14] and they construct aqueducts, those masterpieces of Roman civil engineering and mainstay of urban civilization.

The linking of the signs to various occupations and professions was not peculiar to Manilius. It was actually quite commonplace. One might say indeed that the ancient zodiac furnishes a comprehensive inventory of the work activities of Graeco-Roman society – a fact which has not escaped the notice of social historians.[15] The indexes of editions of astrological authors sometimes provide useful overviews. For Manilius G. P. Goold (1977: 380–1)[16] lists 105 occupations and character types, predominantly the former. For Firmicus Maternus J. Rhys Bram (1975: 315–22) has a separate index for occupations alone: at a rough count, they number about 270. Under the "B," you could become a bandit, barber, bath-attendant, beggar, bird-catcher, bird-seller, bodyguard, botanist, bowman, boxer, bracelet-maker, builder, businessman, or butcher. To judge from the frequency of citation, the stars seem to indicate banditry and business as the most common careers under this letter of the alphabet.

In conclusion, let's listen to a Roman novelist's creation holding forth on this same topic, the signs of the zodiac and what each portends for us. The author is Petronius, his novel is called the *Satyrica*, and he composed it (for oral delivery by a professional reciter trained to represent many different voices) some time before his death in 66 CE. The speaker is Trimalchio, a rich ex-slave of deplorable vulgarity whose wealth can command the attention of his dinner guests to his pretentious ramblings. The topic turns to astrology, or rather is directed that way by a dish with delicacies representing the twelve signs.

"The heavens in which the twelve gods live turn into the same number of figures. Now it becomes a Ram. So anyone who is born in that sign has a lot of flocks and a lot of wool, a hard head, a shameless forehead, and a sharp horn. A lot of scholars and 'ramlets' are born under this sign." We praised the sophistication of our 'mathematical' host, and so he continued. "Then the whole sky becomes a Bullock. So men who kick with their heels are born then, and oxherds and people who feed themselves. In the twins two-horse teams are born, and pairs of oxen, and pairs of balls, and people who plaster and whitewash both sides of a wall. I was born in Cancer the Crab.[17] So I stand on many feet, and I own a lot on sea and land, for things square off nicely both here and there.... In the Lion gluttons and bossy people are born; in Virgo women and runaway slaves and chain-gangs; in Libra butchers and perfumers and anyone who weighs something out; in Scorpio poisoners and murderers; in Sagittarius squinters, people who look at the veggies but make off with the bacon; in Capricorn victims who because of their troubles grow horns; in Aquarius innkeepers and pumpkin-heads; in Pisces cooks and public speakers. So the globe turns like a mill and always does something bad, so that men are either being born or perishing." (*Satyrica* 39)[18]

9 Appendix: Some Omitted Sub-Topics

A self-styled "brief history" of such a complicated subject as astrology has to leave out certain sub-topics, even quite significant ones. Here are brief summaries of the four most important which I have chosen to omit.

(a) The subdivision of the signs of zodiac into thirds or "decans" of 10° each. The decans are of Egyptian origin; they have Egyptian names and are in fact Egyptian gods of mixed anthropomorphic and theriomorphic appearance. On the decans see Bouché-Leclerq 1899: 215–35; Neugebauer and Van Hoesen 1959: 5–6. On the original role of the decans in Egyptian astronomy see Parker 1974 (list of decan names p. 62).

(b) Dodekatemories ("twelfth-parts"). Each sign is divided into equal twelfths of two-and-a-half degrees, and each of these twelfths is allotted to one of the signs in the usual order. The first twelfth of a sign belongs to the sign itself. Thus the first twelfth of Aries belongs to Aries, the second to Taurus, and so on; the first twelfth of Taurus belongs to Taurus, the second to Gemini, and so on. On the dodekatemories see

Bouché-Leclerq 1899: 299–303; Neugebauer and Van Hoesen 1959: 6; Goold 1977: li–lii, on Manilius 2.693–737.

(c) The distribution of parts of the human body to different signs of the zodiac. For astrological purposes the human body has twelve members (or pairs of members), each of which, from head to feet, is allotted to one of the twelve signs in their customary order. Thus Aries gets the head and Pisces the feet. Apart from their application in astrological medicine (iatromathematics), these relationships are important metaphysically, in that together they define a cosmic Man or vice versa they conceptualize Man as a microcosm of the macrocosm. For the complete scheme see (e.g.) Goold 1977: xlvi, on Manilius 2.453–65, 4.704–9 ("Herein for once astrologers find themselves in complete agreement").

(d) Chorography: Different countries and different peoples are allotted to different signs. These allocations are the object of chorography (from the Greek *chôra* = "country"), which is thus a form of astral geography and ethnography combined. The subject is treated at some length by Manilius (4.744–817; see Goold 1977: xci–xcii). Ptolemy (*Tetr.* 2.3) expounds a fuller and more detailed chorography, in that he also factors in the planets and one of the aspects (trine) relating the signs.

6

Structure and Meaning in the Horoscope, 3: The Planets

1 Introduction

Complexity and change – and thus any plausibility that astrology might have in claiming to mirror human life – enters with the planets. So far in the system we have made the acquaintance of two circles, the circle of the twelve places (chapter 4) and the circle of the zodiac with its twelve signs (chapter 5). In both circles the relationship of every sector to every other sector remains the same: the first place is diametrically opposite the seventh place and likewise Aries opposes Libra to all eternity. Of course the circle of the zodiac does rotate once a day against the background of the fixed circle of the places so that every sign occupies every place in succession, but that is the extent of celestial change and variety.

In chapter 3 (section 2) we were introduced to the planets with the metaphor of the seven hands of a clock moving independently against the background of a clock-face calibrated to the twelve signs of the zodiac. These seven hands/planets move at greatly differing speeds counterclockwise (eastwards), the Moon taking a month to complete the circuit, the Sun a year, Mercury and Venus a year on average, Mars just under two years, Jupiter just under twelve years, and Saturn twenty-nine-and-a-half years. The five planets proper, as we saw, interrupt their forward motion with periods of "retrograde" motion, in other words motion clockwise or to the west. This seemingly erratic behavior causes Mercury and Venus, the Sun's close companions, now to dart ahead of the Sun, now to fall behind.

The hands of an ordinary clock do not all turn in the same plane. The minute hand passes in front of the hour hand, and the second hand in front of the minute hand. So it is with planets. On the commonsensical premise that the nearer an object the faster it appears to move, the Greek astronomers placed the Moon's orbit closest to earth,[1] next the orbits of Mercury, Venus, and the Sun (usually in that order), then Mars, then Jupiter, and finally, furthest from earth and closest to the ultimate heaven of the fixed stars, Saturn.

Depth in space was of little practical concern to astrologers. What mattered was the motion in longitude forward and backward, eastward and westward. The complicated passages of the seven planets from sign to sign generated most of the celestial facts on the basis of which horoscopes could be cast. Again, it must be emphasized that statements like "Moon in Taurus on such-and-such a date" are indeed verifiable statements of fact, not astrological fantasies. The fantasies are spun in the subsequent assignment of meaning and value to actual events or "phenomena."

2 Meet the Seven

To start with what is so obvious and fundamental that it is often taken for granted and left unstated: the planets were *gods* – or else the *living* instruments of gods. This means that they were considered agents, in the same sense that human beings are considered agents: they could act and be acted upon in ways comprehensible to us, at least in principle.

One aspect of the planets' life and behavior we can observe and even predict: their motions and their positions relative to one another, to the zodiac, and the horizon. These motions, the ancients assumed, were purposeful, not the mere drifting of inanimate objects from one place to another, and if purposeful, then willed either autonomously or in obedience to some higher intent. In either case the motions could properly be thought significant to humans at the still center on earth around which the divinities wheeled, given that we mortals, in the shared possession of reason, are kin to the gods.

Table 6.1 presents our cast of gods and goddesses. In the first column are the deities with their Latin names. For the five planets proper, these of course are still their names. The next column lists the original Greek deities with whom the Latin deities were equated when the two cultures met and merged. The planets received their Greek names and divine identities when or soon after they were first recognized as a distinct class of "wandering" stars. The impetus to identify the five with those particular gods undoubtedly came from Babylon, as did the alternative divine identities, given in parentheses for Mercury, Venus, and Mars. These alternatives were introduced somewhat later than the principal identities (although still quite early in the history of astrology), and they were never

Table 6.1 The seven planets (from furthest to nearest)

God	Greek name	Descriptive name	Weekday
Saturn	Kronos	Phainon ("shining one")	Saturday
Jupiter	Zeus	Phaëthon ("brilliant one")	Thursday (jeudi)
Mars	Ares (Heracles)	Pyroeis ("fiery one")	Tuesday (mardi)
Sun (Sol)	Helios		Sunday
Venus	Aphrodite (Hera)	Phosphoros ("light-bringer") Hesperos ("evening one")	Friday (vendredi)
Mercury	Hermes (Apollo)	Stilbon ("glittering one")	Wednesday (mercredi)
Moon (Luna)	Selene		Monday

as widely current. They played little or no part in practical genethlialogy. The same is true of the descriptive names in the third column, which Franz Cumont (1935) argued, from their occurrence in certain theoretical works, were intended as neutral, untheological terms coined for scientific ends.[2] Venus is here the exception: *Phôsphoros* (or *Heôsphoros* = dawn-bringer) and *Hesperos* were her original Greek names, alluding to the two aspects of this planet as both Morning Star rising in the east before the Sun and Evening Star setting in the west after the Sun.

In the fourth column are the days of the week over which each planetary god presided, the week itself having its origin at about the beginning of our common era. The order is explained as follows. The first *hour* of the first day (Saturday in antiquity) belongs to the most distant and senior of the planets, Saturn. The next hour is assigned to the next planet, Jupiter, and so on in descending order of distance. The sequence is continuously repeated, with the result that the twenty-fourth hour of the first day falls to Mars and the first hour of the second day, and thus the presidency of that entire day, to the Sun. The rest of the week follows in the familiar order, though the planetary sequence is obscured in English by the substitution of equivalent Germanic gods for the Latin originals preserved in the Romance languages (the French weekday names are here given in parentheses).

The planets acquired their personas from the Greek gods whose manifestations they were. This is true in a primary way of the five, and in a secondary way of the two luminaries, for the Sun acquired some of the traits of Apollo and the Moon some of the traits of Artemis/Diana. Primarily, though, the Sun carries the persona imputed to the Sun god – which is of course a tautology, indicating only that in the ancient world the Sun was divine. Likewise the Moon.

To introduce our cast of planets, I have chosen Vettius Valens, an astrologer writing between 152 and 162 CE, whose work, the *Anthologies*, is preserved in its entirety.[3] Valens in fact begins his work (Book 1, chapter 1) with the planets, introduced in the proper horoscopic sequence beginning with the luminaries (Sun first, Moon second) and then proceeding through the other five in order of distance (Saturn third, Mercury seventh). In heaven, as on earth, precedence matters.

As a practical and theoretical genethlialogist, Valens is concerned with the "influence" of each planet not only on the composite human character but also on the particular activities proper to each planetary type and to success or failure in these activities. In linking a planet to its effects, Valens most frequently uses the verb *sêmainein*, which means "to signify" or, as I prefer to translate it, "to indicate." But he also uses verbs of direct causation (for example, a planet "makes" someone such-and-such a person) or endowment (a planet "gives" someone such-and-such a quality, benefit, or liability).

Here then are Vettius Valens' sketches of the Seven, somewhat abbreviated:

1. The **Sun** is the overseer of all; he is fiery, he is the light of the intellect and the instrument of the soul's perception. In a horoscope he indicates (*sêmainei*) kingship, leadership, intelligence, thought, beauty of form and movement, high fortune, relations with the gods through oracles, judgment, engagement in public affairs, action ... he also indicates the father, the master, friendship, persons of repute, the honor of having one's portrait or statue commissioned and of wearing a crown of office, high-priesthood.... Of the parts of the body, the Sun rules the head, the senses, the right eye, the flanks, the heart ... of materials, gold; of crops, wheat and barley. He is of the diurnal "sect."

2. The **Moon**, who has her being from the reflection of sunlight, thus acquiring a spurious light, indicates human life at birth, the body, the mother ... living together or lawful marriage, nurture ... housekeeping, the queen, the mistress, goods, fortune ... receipts and expenses ... voyages ... living and wandering abroad.... Of the parts of the body she governs the left eye, the stomach, the breasts ... of materials, silver and crystal. She is of the nocturnal "sect."

3. **Saturn** makes those born under him petty, malicious, careworn, self-disparaging, solitary, deceitful ... harsh, downcast, dissemblers, desiccated, robed in black, importunate, miserable.... He causes humiliation, laziness, inactivity, hindrances, long drawn out litigation, reversals, secrets, oppression, fetters, griefs, accusations, tears, loss of parents, captivity, banishment. He makes ... farmers because of his

74

lordship of the soil; also contractors, tax collectors, and men of violence. He brings things to completion; he makes high reputation, distinguished status, executives, custodians, step-fathers. Of materials he governs lead, wood, and stone; of the parts of the body, the legs, the knees ... the kidneys and the internal organs. Of illnesses he is indicative of those that come about through coldness and moisture....[4] He makes people single or widowed, orphaned or childless. He causes violent death in water, by strangulation, in prison, or by dysentery.... He is the star of Nemesis and is of the diurnal "sect."

4. **Jupiter** indicates begetting and offspring, desire, love, alliances, acquaintances, friendships with great men, abundance, salaries, large gifts, good crop yields, justice, rulership, political participation, honors, important religious positions, arbitration at law, credit, inheritances, brotherhood, partnerships, adoptions, security of good things, deliverance from bad things, release from chains, freedom.... Of the parts of the body he governs ... the feet ... the reproductive organs ... the right side of the body. Of materials he governs tin. He is of the diurnal "sect."

5. **Mars** indicates violence, wars, plundering, uproar, excess, adultery ... banishment and flight, alienation of parents, captivity, rape ... falsehoods, empty hopes, robbery with violence ... sundering of friends, anger, battle, insults, enmities, law suits. He also brings about murders, mutilations, bloodshed; attacks of fever, ulcers, blistering, inflammation; imprisonment, tortures; masculinity, perjury, error, negotiations on bad terms; those who work with fire or iron, artisans, masons. He makes military commanders ... the hunt and wild beasts.... Of the parts of the body he governs the head, the fundament, the genitals ... the blood ... of materials he governs iron and cloth (on account of Aries the Ram),[5] wine and legumes. He is of the nocturnal "sect."

6. **Venus** is desire and erotic love. She indicates the mother and the nurturer. She causes ... mirth, friendships, relationships, extra acquisitions of goods, shopping for adornments, reconciliations for good ends, marriages, refined arts and crafts, good singing voices, music, sweetness of melody, beauty of form, painting ... those who love cleanliness and playfulness ... She is the giver of weights and measures, of abundance, of work-places, of giving and taking, of laughter, hilarity,

adornment, and of aquatic creatures. She is the giver of public assistance originating from the womenfolk of the imperial household; she is the [sc. women's] co-worker, and she amplifies the honors from such enterprises. Of the parts of the body she governs the neck and throat, the face, the lips, the organ of smell, ... the union of the sexual organs.... Of materials she governs precious stones and many-colored adornments; of crops, the olive. She is of the nocturnal "sect."

7. **Mercury** indicates education, letters, argumentation, logic, brotherhood, interpretation, embassies, numbers, calculations, geometry, commerce, youth, play, theft, community, messaging, service, profit, discoveries.... He is the giver of discernment and judgment. He is in charge of brothers, younger children, and the skills of advocacy and banking; he also governs temple-builders ... sculptors, doctors, teachers of grammar, lawyers, orators, philosophers, architects, musicians, diviners, sacrificers ... those who use paradox and craftiness in calculations and false arguments ... singers who accompany mimes and those who make their living from display, vagrancy, and unsettled conditions; those who are experts and inquirers concerning celestial phenomena, undertaking that marvelous work with enjoyment and cheerfulness for the glory and profit it brings. [Valens refers of course to his own profession – astrology. There then follows a passage explaining that Mercury allots different professions and destinies according to his ever-changing positions on the zodiac and his aspects to the other planets.] Of the parts of the body he governs, the arms, the shoulders, the fingers ... the hearing ... the tongue; of materials, bronze and all coinage. He governs giving and receiving, for he is the god of the common weal.

3 Benefics and Malefics

How do the planets actually indicate or bring about terrestrial outcomes in their spheres of responsibility. Valens has already sketched an answer in the case of Mercury which he elaborates at the end of his first chapter.

Firstly, it all depends on whether the planet is a "benefic" or a "malefic," for in heaven as on earth there are supposed "good guys" and "bad guys." Secondly, the success or failure of a planet for good or ill depends on his/her power at the given moment (again, as on earth, so in heaven). The planets' powers wax and wane depending on a number of factors, the most crucial of which are (1) their locations on the zodiac, and (2) their aspects to their fellow planets, seen as colleagues or rivals. As always in astrology, the variables are so numerous that a loophole can always be found to reconcile an outcome to a horoscope after the event. However, as a general rule: planets' powers are enhanced when they are well aspected and in signs which are positive for them; they are diminished when they are badly aspected and in signs which are negative for them. But remember that what is good and positive for a benefic is normally the opposite for a malefic and vice versa.

Valens does not explicitly name the benefics and malefics, though in most cases it is fairly obvious from his descriptions which is which. In all sources (to the best of my knowledge) Jupiter and Venus are benefics, Saturn and Mars malefics. The Jupiter–Saturn distinction is the more obvious. Saturn, the "saturnine," is the old, cold, deposed ruler of the gods, jealous, resentful, and introverted. Jupiter is the "jovial" new sovereign, genial and expansive, the benevolent guarantor of rightful power and authority in human institutions. The moral opposition of Venus and Mars, benefic against malefic, is in ways surprising, especially in the male-dominated societies of antiquity. The simple gender opposition – women under Venus, men under Mars – is entirely understandable. Indeed, the two planetary deities have endured as prime gender emblems to this day. But the benefic–malefic classification and Valens' descriptions assert a broader dichotomy: men tend to evil, women tend to good; men destroy, women create; men suffer and inflict pain, women experience and give pleasure; men rape, women's sex is consensual, or at least contractual and within the law. One can perhaps qualify Valens' apparent androphobia by noting that he characterizes Jupiter as a benign antitype to Mars. Jupiter is the just ruler, fostering respect for the laws, right social relationships, and the prosperity which good political rule brings to all, not least the ruler; Mars is the anarchist who subverts the rule of law, plundering and murdering his way to power and the ruin of the commonwealth. Mars enchains; Jupiter liberates. Mars is hatred; Jupiter like Venus is love, but unlike Venus he is male. Within human beings and regardless of gender, Mars, one might say, governs the "ergotropic" (work-oriented) or sympathetic side of the autonomous nervous system; Venus governs the "tropho-tropic" (nurture-oriented) or parasympathetic side.[6]

No malefic is entirely and always bad, just as no benefic is entirely and always good. Saturn, especially, has his positive side. He is the "highest" of the planets and the closest to the sphere of the fixed stars and thus to the ultimate heaven. In myth his rule was often construed as a golden age, lost to Jupiter's celestial coup d'état. Nor did he entirely lose his leadership role. The Babylonian tradition which made him the ruler of the night, as the Sun is the ruler of the day, was dimly remembered in Greek astrology.[7] His connection with agriculture, which is mentioned by Valens but more properly belongs to the Moon as the planet presiding over physical growth, can be explained by his Roman origins as an indigenous god of "sowing."

Mercury is ... well, "mercurial": he is not morally neutral or indif-ferent; rather, he changes sides, depending on the celestial company he happens to be keeping at any given moment.

What then of the two luminaries, the Sun and the Moon? Again, the consensus is not quite what one might expect. The Moon is benefic; the Sun, like Mercury, is intrinsically neither benefic nor malefic. The beneficence of the Moon is unproblematic, but why would the Sun, who is indisputably the leader and orchestrator of his planetary col-leagues be morally ambivalent? Ptolemy (*Tetr.* 1.5) has an explanation or – more likely – an after-the-fact rationalization of this solar ambiva-lence. The planets' powers depend on their physical properties, their heat or their coldness, their dryness or their wetness (1.4). Two of these properties, heat and wetness, are "productive and active"; the other two, coldness and dryness, are "destructive and passive." It follows, then, that "the ancients accepted two of the planets, Jupiter and Venus, together with the Moon, as beneficent because of their tempered nature and because they abound in the hot and the moist, and Saturn and Mars as producing effects of the opposite nature, one because of his excessive cold and the other for his excessive dryness" (1.5, trans. Robbins). The

Sun is certainly hot (good), but he is also "somewhat" dry (bad), while Mercury is alternately dry because of his proximity (in longitude) to the Sun and wet because of his proximity (in depth in space) to the Moon. Consequently, the two of them "join their influences with those of the other planets, with whichever of them they are associated" (1.5). Mercury is opportunistic, but in the Sun's case it is more a matter of a sovereign's beneficence or maleficence depending on the qualities of his courtiers – my speculation, not Ptolemy's, but the metaphor of the shifting politics of the Sun's imperial court was certainly embedded in the Graeco-Roman astrological world view.

To some, especially idealists in the Platonic tradition, the very idea of celestial bodies working evil was repugnant, and in consequence an astrology which postulated planetary malefics as necessary causal agents of evil and suffering was *ipso facto* unacceptable. The great third-century CE Neoplatonist philosopher, Plotinus, attacks this perverse anthropocentric form of astrology, insisting that while the stars might incidentally serve as signs (for those with the wit to read them) each planet "has its own life to itself, and each one's good is in its own act, and has nothing to do with us" (*Ennead* 2.3.3, trans. Armstrong). If they have a common purpose, "we must rather say that the movement of the stars is for the preservation of the whole [i.e. the universe]" (2.3.6).

4 Sun and Moon

The Sun and the Moon, the two "luminaries," are special. Unlike the other five planets, they are visibly extended objects, not dimensionless points of light. In appearance they are disks, each approximately half a degree in angular diameter. From their two-dimensional appearance Greek astronomers correctly inferred that they are in fact spheres. They also figured out that the Moon is smaller than the earth in volume and the Sun many times larger. The mean distance of the Moon from the earth was established at 59 earth radii, quite close to the actual value of 60.4. Determining the Sun's true distance was then impossible, but at least the ancients knew on valid grounds that it was many, many times the earth–moon distance. The Sun's brilliant disk gives no intimation of its actual composition, though "fire" (with an admixture of air) would be a reasonable commonsensical guess within the framework of the ancient four-element system. However, it would have to be a very special form of fire with the property, nowhere encountered on earth but ubiquitous in heaven, of moving always and only in a circle. In contrast, the Moon has readily visible features in the form of lighter and darker areas, so speculation about her topography as an earthlike and possibly inhabitable body was not unreasonable.[8]

Most important from an astrological perspective are the manifest causal effects of the Sun and Moon on life on earth. The Sun is the ultimate source of light and heat, of day and night, of the cycle of the seasons, and thus of life and growth. Less obviously, the Moon governs the tides and the female menstrual cycle. Her phases, from new moon to full moon and back to new, furnish the most dramatic of the measures of time. Arguing from the undeniable effects of the luminaries the astrologers by analogy postulated causal agency for the other five planets. This was the route taken by Ptolemy in the *Tetrabiblos* (1.2–10), using, as we saw above, a logic of planetary qualities based on the four fundamental properties of heat, cold, dryness, and moisture. The problem is not the logic of the enterprise, which is impeccable, but the deduction of "facts" from *a priori* physical principles where what is really called for is *induction* from observed cause-and-effect relationships. Astrology is not the sleep of reason but reason hyperactively spinning its wheels.

While Zeus/Jupiter is king and father of gods and men on earth, the Sun is the undisputed sovereign of the planetary heavens. His orbit, the ecliptic, is the median planetary path, from which the others may deviate, but never he. In depth of space he is midway between earth at the center and the sphere of the fixed stars at the outer limit of the universe. In standard cosmology three planets lie below him (Moon, Mercury, Venus) and three above (Mars, Jupiter, Saturn). Aptly he is termed the "leader, the prince, the moderator of the other lights" (Cicero, *Scipio's Dream* 4.2 – see Stahl 1952: 73). Visibly he orchestrates their dance,[9] and by inference from appearances he is the principle of intelligence behind it. Hence he is "the mind and organizing agent of the universe" (Cicero, ibid.).

Since he is also the ultimate light of the universe, he governs that by which we can discern the universe, perception.

Astrologically, the Moon is concerned above all with physical being and growth, in plants, animals, and humans. She is thus the primary governor of agriculture and animal husbandry, of the very means of human life itself. "Of the two faculties identified with terrestrial bodies," says the polymath Macrobius at the turn of the fourth and fifth centuries CE, "sense-perception and growth, the first comes from the Sun, the second from the Moon" (*Commentary on Scipio's Dream* 1.19.23 – see Stahl 1952: 167).

Although essentially benefic, the Moon has her negative side. With her mottled appearance and her notorious mutability (relatively rapid changes of speed, waxing and waning, considerable deviation from the ecliptic) she seems the least "perfect" of the planets. And in fact her orbit came to be considered the boundary between the harmonious and immutable order of heaven and the mutability and decay of our (literally) "sublunar" world. The Moon herself guards the frontier, for she is Persephone too, Queen of Hades, which some thought lay not in an underworld but in a liminal zone above. All planets direct or indicate Fate, but the changeable Moon seems to personify its fluctuations.

5 Celestial Outfitters

The planets govern our physical and psychological make-up in a more direct way than by "influence" beamed down remotely from their spheres. Popular in late Graeco-Roman times were narratives of the descent and return of the soul from the sphere of the fixed stars down to earth and back again. These accounts were meant to be read literally as actual soul-journeys in which the descending soul acquires from each planet in succession the constituents of its mortal being and surrenders them at death in reverse order as it ascends back to heaven.[10] The narrative serves a psychological purpose, of obvious concern to astrologers: to explain by analysis into specific functions why we humans are such strange and conflicted bundles of reason, passion, desires, and emotions.

A brief passage from Macrobius' *Commentary on Scipio's Dream* illustrates this story of the outfitting of the nascent human soul. From the planets, says Macrobius, the descending soul

> acquires each of the attributes which it will exercise later. In the sphere of Saturn it obtains reason and understanding, called *logistikon* and *theoretikon*; in Jupiter's sphere, the power to act, called *praktikon*; in Mars' sphere a bold spirit or *thymikon*; in the sun's sphere, sense-perception and imagination, *aisthetikon* and *phantastikon*; in Venus' sphere, the impulse of passion, *epithymetikon*; in Mercury's sphere, the ability to speak and interpret, *hermeneutikon*; and in the lunar sphere, the function of molding and increasing bodies, *phytikon*. (*Commentary* 1.12.13–14, trans. Stahl 1952: 136 – the untranslated Greek terms are original to Macrobius, embedded in his Latin text)

An alternative narrative of descent and ascent restricted the stations of acquisition and surrender to the two luminaries. In the version given by Plutarch in his essay *On the Face in the Moon* (see note 8, above) the mind is the gift of the Sun and the soul, as the animating principle, the gift of the Moon. The Moon is further associated with the whole process of descent and coming into being or "genesis," and the Sun with ascent and departure from the world of mortality or "apogenesis." Interestingly, the Sun in this scenario has undergone an inversion. From the source of light and warmth and thus of life itself, he has become the source of burning heat which desiccates and consumes. But the life he destroys is *physical* life. The rational mind he liberates.[11]

6 "Sects" and Gender

In our overview of the individual planets you will have noticed one unexplained technical term. Towards the end of the characterization Vettius assigned each planet either to the "diurnal sect" or to the "nocturnal sect." The Greek word translated "sect" (*hairesis*) means literally a "choice," hence a choice of one side over another, hence a school of philosophy, a faction, party, or sect (pejoratively, a "heresy").

The planets, then, take sides. Following the Sun in the day-time/diurnal sect are Saturn and Jupiter; following the Moon in the night-time/ nocturnal sect are Mars and Venus. Mercury, as befits his mercurial character, keeps faith with neither. Note that these alliances do not replicate the division between benefics and malefics.[12]

A more obvious and more fundamental distinction is that between genders. In chapter 5 we saw how an artificial system of alternating male and female signs was imposed on the zodiac, with the bizarre result that a male Ram necessitated a female Bull. For the planets common sense prevailed over structure and balance. Five of the planets are ineluctably male, though the group could be reduced by making the changeable Mercury bisexual (hermaphrodite). The remaining two, the Moon and Venus, are ineluctably female.

To redress the imbalance, astrology resorted to the interesting expedient of allowing the planets, in defined circumstances, to modify their gender. A male planet could be "feminized" and a female planet "made masculine." By the same token, the maleness of a male planet could be reinforced; likewise the femininity of a female planet. It would be a mistake to attribute this modification entirely to the astrologers' need for strategies to explain away awkward outcomes. To some extent, I think, it recognizes the reality that gender is more than just a physiological given. Gender, to put it in postmodern terms, is also constructed and conditioned culturally.

The basic gender of a planet was thought to be a function of the predominance of dryness (male) or wetness (female). Gender could be modified or reinforced by any of three factors: (1) The sign of the zodiac occupied: male signs masculinize, female signs feminize. (2) Aspect to the Sun: preceding the rising Sun masculinizes, following the setting Sun feminizes. (3) The quadrant of the circle of places occupied: ascendant to midheaven masculinizes (the planet dries out, as it were, from the nocturnal moistures of the preceding quadrant), as does descendant to lower midheaven; the other two quadrants (midheaven to descendant and lower midheaven to ascendant) feminize.

According to Antiochus of Athens (*CCAG* 1.145.12–22, transmitted through a later astrologer, Rhetorius), the effects of the enhancement and moderation of planetary gender on the human character is as follows:

Masculinized planets in masculine signs or quadrants contribute to masculine nativities. They make men headstrong, rash, possessed of masculinity; women they make undignified, shameless, rash, insubordinate, male in sexual orientation. Feminized planets ... make men soft, tenderhearted, timid and fearful, eunuchs, and those engaged in women's work; women they make self-effacing, modest, sensible, respectable, properly subordinate to their menfolk, versed in women's customs.

The moral: enhancement of femininity good, enhancement of masculinity not so good, masculinizing the female and feminizing the male bad.

Here, to generalize, is a good example of astrology's modeling of the complex human make-up on an analytical grid. Seemingly contradictory characteristics are located and explained by reference to location on the grid. As so often, the structure is binary: nativity of a boy or girl? planetary god or goddess? planet currently masculinized or feminized? From our point of view, it is the construction of the character grid itself that is of interest, not the absurd predictive purposes to which it was put. Note finally, that the grid has normative as well as descriptive intent. It plots out not only the way things are in human gendering but also the way they should and should not be. In terms of Clifford Geertz's cultural anthropology (1973: 93–4), it is both a "model of" and "model for" masculinity and femininity.

7 Power and Weakness, Friends and Enemies: Houses, Exaltations, Humiliations, Terms

The strife and uneasy alliances among the signs of the zodiac, which we looked at in the preceding chapter (section 7), are more than replicated among the planets. What philosophical cosmologists saw as a beautifully orchestrated dance seemed to the astrologers at best the maneuverings of an imperial court – as on earth, so in heaven – and at worst all-out war. Power was what it was all about; and power was a function of place, of being in the right place with well-placed allies and disadvantaged enemies.

The planets all had their own "houses,"[13] their own "exaltations," and their own "humiliations,"[14] each in different signs of the zodiac In their houses and exaltations they were strong, in their humiliations weak. The planetary houses, exaltations, and humiliations are displayed in table 6.2.

The older of the two systems is that of exaltations and humiliations, which is now known to be of Babylonian origin (Rochberg-Halton 1988: 53–7). Note that the humiliation of a planet is diametrically opposite the exaltation. The system of houses clearly shows Greek structural logic at work. The intent is to allocate all the signs of the zodiac among the planets without remainder. The problem of course is that seven is not a factor of twelve. The solution is to allocate one sign to each of the two luminaries and two to each of the five other planets. Leo was assigned to the Sun and Cancer to the Moon. The five signs forward from Leo were then assigned to the five non-luminaries in order of distance from the earth (nearest to farthest), and the five signs backward from Cancer to the same five in the same order. The non-luminaries thus have both day-time houses (Virgo forward to Capricorn) and night-time houses (Gemini backward to Aquarius).

Why these particular allocations? Antiochus (*CCAG* 1.147–8) furnishes an ingenious *ex post facto* rationale which suggests further lines of interpretation and meaning. He starts with the fact that the planets are paired in their exaltations and humiliations (cf. table 6.2). In each pair the exaltation of one is the humiliation of the other:

Table 6.2   The "houses," "exaltations," and "humiliations" of the planets

Planet	House (diurnal)	House (nocturnal)	Exaltation	Humiliation
Sun	Leo ⇐		Aries (19°)	Libra (19°)
Moon		Cancer	Taurus (3°)	Scorpius (3°)
Mercury	Virgo	Gemini	Virgo (15°)	Pisces (15°)
Venus	Libra ⇓ ⇑	Taurus	Pisces (27°)	Virgo (27°)
Mars	Scorpius	Aries	Capricorn (28°)	Cancer (28°)
Jupiter	Sagittarius	Pisces	Cancer (15°)	Capricorn (15°)
Saturn	Capricorn ⇐	Aquarius	Libra (21°)	Aries (21°)

Why where the Sun is exalted, there Saturn is humiliated, and where Saturn is exalted, there the Sun is humiliated? We say that the Sun is the store of fire and light and the lord of day and that Saturn is cold and indicates darkness; so where the light of day is exalted, there darkness and night are humiliated and the cold is warmed [and vice versa]. Again, why where Jupiter is exalted, there Mars is humiliated, and where Mars is exalted, there Jupiter is humiliated? We say that Jupiter is the overseer of the breath of life and of abundance and that Mars is the overseer of death; so where the breath of life increases, there the quality of death is lowered [and vice versa]. Again, why where Venus is exalted, there Mercury is humiliated, and where Mercury is exalted, there Venus is humiliated? We say that Mercury is the lord of reason and Venus the overseer of desire and sex; so where reason increases, there the desire and pleasure of sex is lowered [and vice versa]. Again, why where the Moon is exalted, there no one is humiliated, and where the Moon is humiliated no one is exalted? We say that the Moon is the fortune of the whole, and whom fortune exalts no one humiliates and whom fortune humiliates no one exalts. (147.24–148.15)

The houses (cf. table 6.2) Antiochus explicates as follows:

Why are the houses of the Sun and the Moon opposite the houses of Saturn? We say that the Sun and the Moon are the luminaries of the universe and that Saturn is the lord of darkness: thus light always opposes darkness and darkness light. Again, why are the houses of Mercury opposite the houses of Jupiter [and vice versa]? We say that Jupiter is the overseer of assets and prosperity and Mercury is always the lord of reason: thus reason always opposes and despises the desire for assets, and prosperity is opposed to reason [sic!]. Again, why are the houses of Mars opposed to the houses of Venus? We say that Venus is the overseer of all desire and enjoyment and pleasure and Mars of all fear and war and wrath. So the enjoyable, the desirous, and the pleasurable is opposed to the fearful, the wrathful, and the martial. (148.16–29)

"Opposition" is the key term here: being on opposite sides of the zodiac translates into both contrary characteristics and confrontation.

Greek astrology spawned a plethora of other devices by which, for good or ill, the powers of the planets relative to each other might be enhanced or diminished. The most mathematical of these was the system of "terms," in which sub sectors of the zodiac below the level of complete signs were assigned to different planets (Bouché-Leclercq 1899: 206–15; N&VH 12). Planets also "guarded" (literally, "spear-carried for") each other in various elaborately defined circumstances (Bouché-Leclercq 1899: 252–4). They had their "proper faces," their "chariots," and their "thrones" (Ptolemy, *Tetr.* 1.23). The list is inexhaustible, but as Bouché-Leclercq sadly observed (254) enmity in the Greek astrological cosmos generally outweighs "politesse."

8 On the Road: The Planets in N&VH no. 81

To recapture something of the sense of drama latent in the dry particulars of planetary longitudes in run-of-the-mill Greek horoscopes, I shall conclude this chapter on the planets with a translation of one of the "deluxe" horoscopes from Neugebauer and Van Hoesen's collection, no. 81.[15] Presumably, you paid considerably more for a deluxe than for a standard horoscope. Part of what you got for your money was greater detail in the calculations and more elaborate astrological trimmings. But you also got a more elevated and imaginative rhetoric. N&VH 81 presents the horoscope as a moment in the narrative of the Progress of the Planets, a celestial pageant fraught with grandeur and high intent.

> The Egyptian men of old who lawfully studied the heavenly bodies and learned the motions of the seven gods, compiled and arranged everything in perpetual tables and generously left to us their knowledge of these things. From these I have accurately calculated ... each one according to degree and minute, aspect and phase.... For thus the way of astrological prediction is made straight and unambiguous, that is consistent. Farewell, dearest Hermon.
>
> Time ... the third year of the Divine Titus, the sixth day of Pharmouthi, the third hour of the night; as the Romans reckon, the Kalends of April[16] ...

Hence the Sun, the very greatest and ruler of all, advancing from the spring equinox had reached in Aries fourteen degrees and six minutes ... in the sign [i.e. house] of Mars; in the terms of Mercury; ... in exaltation in a male and northerly sign; shining upon the flank of Aries;[17] in the second decan, called Sentachor; the dodekatemorion[18] was illuminating the First Joint [i.e. of the tail] of Scorpio.

And the divine and light-bringing Moon, in her first quarter, had covered in Taurus thirteen degrees and a thousandth part of a degree; in the sign [house] of Venus; in her own exaltation; in the terms of Mercury; in a female and solid sign; like gold; mounting (*anabibazousa*) the back of Taurus;[19] in the second decan called Aroth; its dodekatemorion was shining on about the same place in Scorpio.

And Phainon, the star of Saturn, had completed six degrees in Pisces, lacking a sixtieth of a degree, in the sign [house] of Jupiter, in the terms and the exaltation of Venus; at his morning rising;[20] descending (*katabibazôn*) from the Swallow-Fish;[21] ...

And Phaethon, the star of Jupiter, traversing his exaltation in Cancer, had reached six degrees and ten sixtieths of the third order [i.e. $10/60^3$] which are one 21,600th part of a degree; in the sign [house] of the Moon; in the terms and humiliation of Mars; ... two fingers [i.e. $2 \times 1/12°$] north of the bright star on the back [of Cancer]; ...

And Pyroeis, the star of Mars, had climbed in Aquarius, the sign [house] of Saturn, sixteen degrees and a twentieth; the triangle of Mercury; the terms of Jupiter; [by] the star in the cloak, called Ganymede, homonymous with the whole constellation;[22] rising well before dawn.

And Phosphoros, the star of Venus, had completed in Pisces sixteen degrees and four minutes ... in the sign [house] of Jupiter; in her own exaltation; rising at dawn; at the Southern Fish; like crystal; in the terms of Mercury; distant two lunar diameters from the star in the Connecting Cords.[23]

And Stilbon, the star of Mercury, had run in Aries ten full degrees; at perigee; having completed its phase before the seventh; therefore it will dominate the configuration.[24]

And the rudder of them all, the Horoscopos, has cut off eighteen degrees in Scorpio; the terms of Mercury; the sign [house] of Mars; the triangle of the moon; the decan Thoumouth.

88

> And the meridian at right angles to this [i.e. the midheaven] had struck the back of the Lion.
> And the lot of fortune[25] ... will be in the sign [house] of Jupiter [i.e. Sagittarius] and in his triangle ...
> Good luck!
> Titus Pitenius computed it as is set forth.

Bear in mind that from start to finish this is a construct of the imagination. Of course Pitenius did not arbitrarily invent the positions of the planets; rather, as he himself acknowledged in the preamble, he reconstructed them from the "perpetual tables."[26] From the rows and columns of the tables Pitenius envisaged the positions and relationships of the "divine" planets as they went about their business at the moment of Hermon's birth, in all likelihood some twenty or thirty years before. Perhaps Pitenius imagined the celestial scene, in whole or as a composite of frames, in his mind's eye. If so, he was replicating or re-representing to himself a scene or scenes accessible only to an ideal observer capable of viewing the sky below the horizon and the planets in full sunlight. But the astrologer's principal act of imagination is to represent the planets not as moving *objects* but as purposeful *agents* who in their travels unceasingly modify and recalibrate heaven's balance of power.

9 Appendix: The "Lots"

Towards the end of N&VH 81, after identifying the signs occupied by the *horoscopos* and the midheaven, Pitenius identifies the position of the "lot of fortune," namely Sagittarius qua house of Jupiter. The lots – there are seven them, of which the lot of fortune is the most important – are the penultimate second-order constructs of which we need to take note (the last being the "starter" and "destroyer" which we shall look at in chapter 8). They are points of significance on the zodiac determined by various formulas from the positions of the *horoscopos* and the planets, especially the Sun and the Moon (N&VH pp. 8–9). The position of the lot of fortune is determined by adding the elongation of the Moon from the Sun to the longitude of the *horoscopos*. In N&VH 81 the Moon is twenty-nine degrees distant from the Sun and the *horoscopos* is at Scorpio 18°. The lot of fortune is accordingly in Sagittarius (Scorpio 18° + 29° = Sagittarius 17°). Those who subtract, putting the lot back in Libra, do so "out of ignorance," adds Pitenius.

7

Horoscopes and Their Interpretation

1 The Handbooks

So what did fate hold in store for Hermon whose horoscope, as we saw at the end of the preceding chapter, was so painstakingly reconstructed by Titus Pitenius? Pitenius, like virtually all practicing astrologers, does not commit himself, at least not on the same piece of papyrus.

Where then should we turn? The astrological handbooks? If not for Hermon in particular, then surely that is where we shall find the principles and procedures which will lead us from any given celestial configuration to its implied outcome in the life of the human subject, the horoscope's "native."

Unfortunately, not so. As practical aids to discovering straightforward and unambiguous outcomes (X will happen, not Y) the handbooks are useless. In an elegant experiment in chapter 5 of her *Ancient Astrology* (1994: 114–42) Tamsyn Barton systematically tested the configurations in the horoscope of Charles, Prince of Wales, against the outcomes predicted for these configurations by two ancient authorities, Dorotheus of Sidon who wrote in the first century CE and Firmicus Maternus who wrote in the fourth. The problem was not that these authors furnished *wrong* predictions for Charles's life to date, but that they furnished a mass of *contradictory* outcomes. Charitably, and I think rightly, Barton concluded that Dorotheus and Firmicus were not deliberately hedging their bets so as to allow the practitioner to reconcile retrospectively any set of data with any outcome. Rather, she claims (again rightly in my view) that the handbooks served an altogether different purpose. They were not do-it-yourself manuals; they were show pieces, designed to exhibit the depth and detail of the masters' knowledge. In any case, astrology was and is an art, not a science to be mastered by book-learning. You can no more learn to interpret a horoscope with skill and insight from a manual than you can learn to drive a car from the same sort of written source. Driving and genethlialogy are equally hands-on skills.

The handbooks, then, give *too much* information on possible outcomes, not *too little*. I want to suggest a further reason for this superabundance of cause-and-effect relationships in the astrological literature over and above exhibitionism on the one hand or the construction of a fail-safe system on the other. Each horoscope, in the sense of each configuration of the heavens at a particular birth, is comprised of a large number of relationships which obtain between celestial entities of different types (planets, signs, places/centers). Subject to certain constraints (e.g. the close attendance of Mercury and Venus on the Sun), each of the seven planets can be found in any aspect to any other planet. The aspected planets, for example Venus in quartile aspect to Mars, can be found in any pair of signs which are themselves in quartile aspect to each other (e.g. in Taurus and Leo). The signs and the planets together revolve daily against the fixed circle of the twelve places; consequently, any sign and any planet can occupy any place, provided only that they do so in the proper sequence. Lastly we must factor in a whole host of other relationships generated by second-order constructs such as the terms, the lots, and the dodekatemories. Clearly the total number of relationships, each of which carries its own significance for good or ill, is very large indeed. While not infinite, the number of relationships and hence the number of predictable meanings which can be read into a horoscope is in practice inexhaustible.

So let us think of a horoscope as a large bundle of celestial relationships each of which correlates with one or more outcomes in the life of the native. But at the moment of birth these are only potential outcomes. They *may* occur; the native *may* develop such-and-such a disposition, *may* engage in such-and-such a career. Much, as astrologers such as Ptolemy admitted, will depend on circumstance. Only when the life is lived and over can we assess with certainty the actual outcomes, distinguishing those which were realized from those which were not. Only then can we identify with certainty those few celestial relationships in the horoscope's total configuration which (*ex hypothesi*) signaled or caused outcomes.

The astrologer's art (granting for the sake of the argument the validity of its causal and/or semantic assumptions) is to identify those celestial relationships in a horoscope which are likely to lead to outcomes and to discern there from the nature of the outcomes signified. It is like the proverbial search for needles in a haystack – only at a stage when the needles are still just wisps of straw like all the others.

Interpretive superabundance was not built into astrology by design. It evolved with the system itself. Nevertheless, it is surely a necessary property for a system which pretends to mirror all the complexities and contingencies of human life. It is the lack of it which makes, for example, Sun sign horoscopes so implausible: as if each twelfth of the world's population shared a common daily fortune depending solely on the longitude of the Sun at birth!

2 Post-Mortem Analysis: Matching Configurations with Actual Outcomes

There is one class of horoscope extant in which configurations are indeed matched with outcomes: the horoscopes of dead natives. There outcomes are indeed outcomes, and "prediction" is an exercise in postulating celestial causes for actual events.

The horoscopes of the dead were of interest to professional astrologers first because they afforded an empirical check on outcomes and secondly so as to postulate supposedly "real" cause and effect relationships. Interpretive superabundance, built into the system, would ensure that for any and every outcome there would be more than enough celestial relationships within a horoscope's configurations to furnish plausible explanations of why things turned out the way they did.

The extant Greek horoscopes of this type are presented by Neugebauer and Van Hoesen in chronological sequence separately from the "original" horoscopes. They are termed "literary" horoscopes, and their date-numbers are prefixed L. Their most copious source is Vettius Valens, whose *Anthologies* furnish about four-fifths of the entire literary set. The earliest birth date in the Valens horoscopes is 37 CE, the latest is 173,[1] and the densest period is roughly the first quarter of the second century. After the Valens set the literary record is silent for over two hundred years, resuming with L380, a singleton from Hephaestion of (Egyptian) Thebes which happens to be his own horoscope (*Apotelesmatica* 2.2, 1.91.27 ed. Pingree).

The earliest literary horoscopes, L–71 and L–42, are a pair from the famous astrologer-politician Ti. Claudius Balbillus (first century CE), about which and about whom we shall hear more later, for these horoscopes raise the dangerous topic of the "starter" and the "destroyer," the stars in charge of launching and terminating a life. The latest horoscope is L621. It is not a personal horoscope, but rather the horoscope of a collective, in this instance the "nation" (*ethnos*) of Islam. It takes as the equivalent of the moment of birth the third hour (about 9:00 a.m.) on September 1, 621, the first day of the Byzantine year in which the *hijra* (Muhammad's move from Mecca to Medina, July 16, 622) took place. The predictions are astonishingly accurate until the year 775, when they peter out into mere "wishful thinking" (N&VH). The wishful thinking is that of an eighth-century Byzantine, for whom the advent of Islam had meant the loss of most of the Asian provinces of the Roman empire, already restricted to the eastern half of the old empire. The obvious inference to be made is that the horoscope itself was constructed about a century and a half after its purported date, although "Stephanus," the author-astrologer, constructs a *mise en scène* in which he hears about the coming of the prophet *Môamed* from an

Arabian merchant friend at a time when the Islamic conquests still lie in the future. The bravery and enterprise of the new "nation" are emphasized: "... outstanding in great strength and unrestrained speed and constant motion and of enduring possession, with epic battles and most brilliant deeds of valor and distinguished by a new type of state" (N&VH trans.). We shall return to L621 later in this chapter. Apart from its inherent interest at the start of the third millennium when people who should know better are again raising the specter of the "clash of civilizations," it illuminates exceptionally well the technical methods by which a sophisticated Greek astrologer could unpack, as it were, an entire history, whether personal or institutional, from the configuration of the heavens at a given initial moment.

Among the most interesting literary horoscopes are a set of three (L40, L76, L113.IV)[2] attributed by Hephaestion to an earlier astrologer, Antigonus of Nicaea. L76 is the horoscope of the emperor Hadrian (ruled 117–38), while the other two belong, one to an older family member of his family, either his father or his uncle, the other to a younger member who came to a bad end, probably Pedanius Fuscus who was put to death by Hadrian for conspiracy and treason, although there are some chronological difficulties with this identification. In the next chapter we shall return to Hadrian's horoscope to see what it is in a person's horoscope that destines him for empire.

A rarity among literary horoscopes, L484 addresses wrong predictions actually made. L484 is a catarchic horoscope, in other words an attempt to determine astrologically a favorable moment for a given undertaking. The undertaking of 484 was the coronation of a usurping emperor, Leontius. The coup subsequently failed. Obviously Leontius' astrologers – there were two of them – had failed to read the stars correctly. Some time later a third astrologer, Palchus (of uncertain date) or his source, analyzed the horoscope and pinpointed the negative factors which his predecessors had failed to take into account. For example, "they did not turn (their attention) first to (the fact that) Mercury (in Leo), the ruler of the day and hour, had fallen into passivity, for it had its greatest elongation from the sun and was in aspect only to Saturn (in Scorpio). And this indicates violent death" (trans. N&VH).

95

The logic, both explicit and implicit, of the reinterpretation goes something like this: Mercury was important, because the coronation was set for a Wednesday, the day which, and the first hour of which, Mercury rules. But Mercury had turned passive. So the most important planet in the horoscope was ineffective, and that was bad news. Why had Mercury turned passive? Because he was at maximum elongation from the Sun, which somehow weakened him. Furthermore, he was in aspect only to Saturn, and Saturn is almost always bad news. So is Scorpio, the sign in which Saturn was then found. Moreover, the aspect here was quadrature, and quadrature is likewise negative. The entailment of all these factors? Violent death.

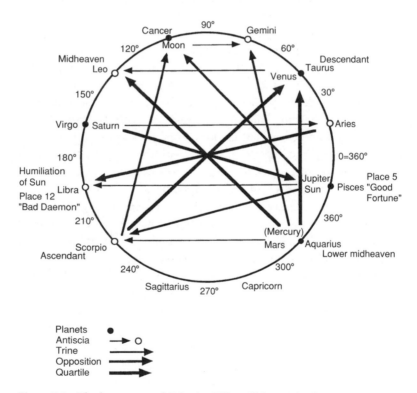

Figure 7.1 The horoscope of Ceionius Rifius Albinus. Firmicus Maternus, *Mathesis* 2.29.10–20. March 14, 303 CE, about 10.00 p.m.

How could Leontius' astrologers have been so incompetent as to miss these sinister factors? The answer is that in any horoscope there are hundreds of first- or second-order astronomical/astrological relationships between the celestial elements of the horoscope. After the event, it is easy enough to single out or combine these relationships into strings of causal factors with sinister implications – or with beneficial implications if an unexpectedly fortunate outcome has followed a superficially gloomy configuration of the stars. The operative factors are obvious only in hindsight; before that they were mere potentialities among innumerable others.

Catarchic horoscopes are the easiest to assess retrospectively, since they are aimed at a single desired outcome (either it worked or it didn't work) rather than the outcomes of an entire life as is the case with birth horoscopes. As our first major example of a birth horoscope analyzed retrospectively I have selected that found in Firmicus Maternus, *Mathesis* 2.29. It is not included in the Neugebauer and Van Hoesen collection, for the sole reason that its language is Latin. In all other respects it is indistinguishable from a "Greek horoscope," and Firmicus goes out of his way to specify the Greek pedigree of the theory which his analysis of the horoscope illustrates (2.29.2).[3] The horoscope is displayed diagrammatically in figure 7.1.

3 An Example: Firmicus Maternus and the Horoscope of "You Know Who"

As we noted in chapter 5 (section 6), what Firmicus discusses in *Mathesis* 2.29 is the theory of "antiscia" ("counter-shadows") according to which a planet may project a proxy of itself across the zodiac to a sign or even to a precise degree of a sign with the same rising time. Thus a planet in Taurus, for example, may send an antiscium into Leo; or, more precisely, a planet in the tenth degree of Taurus into the twentieth of Leo. Diagrammatically, in figure 3.1 antiscia are sent along horizontal lines, in other words lines parallel to the line connecting the equinoxes.

Generally speaking, nice planets project nice antiscia and nasty planets nasty antiscia. However, the antiscia themselves generate a whole new set of aspects and engage different signs which may or may not be sympathetic to the originating planets. So the antiscia are the wild cards in the astrological deck, and, says Firmicus, you can't watch them too carefully.

> How much the force of the antiscia counts and how effectively the theory of the antiscia works you will be able to learn from this nativity which we are about to give: this man had a chart with the Sun in Pisces, the Moon in Cancer, Saturn in Virgo, Jupiter in Pisces in the same degree as the Sun, Mars in Aquarius, Venus in Taurus, Mercury in Aquarius in the same degree as Mars, the ascendant in Scorpio. The father of this native after a pair of consulships was sent into exile, and the native himself was exiled for the crime of adultery. He was suddenly brought back from exile and was chosen for the administration of Campania, then the proconsulship of Achaia (Greece), and afterwards was made proconsul of Africa and Prefect of the City of Rome. (2.29.10, trans. Rhys Bram, with a few minor changes and corrections)

"Whose horoscope this is, you know very well," adds Firmicus, addressing his patron and the dedicatee of his work, "our distinguished Lollianus" (2.29.10). The biography fits not Lollianus but another Roman nobleman, Ceionius Rufius Albinus, who is now accepted as the "native" of the horoscope (Neugebauer 1953).

Superficially, the horoscope appears benign, so benign that

> any man not knowing the theory of the antiscia, if he saw the Sun with Jupiter in the same degree in the fifth place from the ascendant – that is in the place of Good Fortune – ... would have foretold a father fortunate, prosperous, powerful, and so on, and the same thing for the native himself. Concerning his exile and the constant plots against him he would have been able to foretell nothing unless he turned his attention to the theory of the antiscia. (2.29.11, trans. Rhys Bram, as above)

The set-backs, then, are latent in the horoscope, though at a deeper level accessible to a true professional. They are as follows (2.29.12–19):

1. The Sun and Jupiter send their antiscium from Pisces into Libra. But Libra is the humiliation of the Sun (strike one!), and Libra is in the twelfth place, the place of the Bad Daemon (strike two!). "This shows a humble origin for the father and determines for the father himself a scandalous exile"; also numerous and effective enemies for both father and son.

2. Saturn in Virgo is in opposition to the Sun in Pisces (strike three! – Saturn is a malefic and opposition is a bad aspect). Saturn sends his antiscium from Virgo into Aries. Saturn's antiscium in Aries is in opposition to the Sun's in Libra (next batter – strike one!). This was another cause of the father's exile.

3. The Moon in Cancer sends her antiscium into Gemini. Mars in Aquarius "looks at" this lunar antiscium on his right. Mars in aspect to the waxing Moon, whether to the right or left, is "pernicious" (strike two!).[4] This factor helps to explain the native's own exile, the charge of adultery, and some health problems.

4. Mars in Aquarius sends his antiscium into Scorpio. Scorpio is the rising sign and Aquarius is the sign at lower midheaven. So Mars in projecting his antiscium is attacking ("struck with violent ray") the ascendant, which is the "prime degree of life" (strike three!).

5. Mars' antiscium in Scorpio is in trine aspect to the Moon in Cancer (third batter – strike one!).

And so it goes. "The waxing Moon, assaulted from ambushes on every side by the rays of Mars, overwhelmed the native with many illnesses and eventually sent him into exile" (2.29.16). But all is not lost – Jupiter to the rescue! "And had not Jupiter in Pisces regarded the ascendant in trine aspect, the native would never have been freed from exile. And had not Jupiter also regarded the Moon in trine aspect in his own house (for Cancer is the exaltation of Jupiter), he would have died a violent death."

Even so, the perils of the horoscope are not exhausted. To explain the adultery, Firmicus points out (2.29.17) that

6. Mars' antiscium in Scorpio is in opposition to Venus in Taurus (third batter – strike two!). Compounding the danger is the fact that Scorpio and Mars' antiscium are rising in the ascendant and Venus and Taurus setting in the descendant (strike three!).

7. Furthermore, Venus sends her antiscium into Leo, where it is threatened by Mars in opposition in Aquarius (fourth batter – strike one!).

8. Finally, Venus is directly threatened by Mars, planet to planet without intermediary antiscia. She is in Taurus and he is in Aquarius and those two signs are in quadrature, another bad aspect (strike two!).

As Firmicus sums it up, "in every way, both by themselves and through their antiscia on the centres of the nativity [i.e. the ascendant, etc.], Venus and Mars, either in opposition or in quadrature, attacked each other with [literally!] an unfriendly sort of association." Clearly, bad sex in some form is indicated. "This configuration made the native criminally liable for adultery."

The case was heard by the emperor himself. Does anything in the horoscope foretell that? Yes – as we saw above (configuration no. 7), Venus sends her antiscium into Leo. Leo is the house of the Sun and indicates royalty, a significance reinforced by its position at midheaven in the horoscope (2.29.18).

This is still not the end of Firmicus' analysis, but it is perhaps close to the end of the reader's patience. So I will merely touch on the roles (a) of Mercury and Saturn – located in each other's houses they made the native "an expert in arcane literature" and "rhetorically and stylistically worthy of comparison with the authors of old" – and (b) of the Moon: located in her own house and in the ninth place ("God"), "she had the chief power to determine high honours and offices" for the native (2.29.18–19).

What do we learn from Firmicus' matching of the horoscope and life of his – and his patron's – acquaintance Ceionius Rufius Albinus? Perhaps the most important finding is the sheer size of the reservoir of celestial configurations and relationships in a horoscope – any horoscope – on which a professional astrologer can draw. Each configuration and each relationship is potentially a causal factor in a client's life. The astrologer works abductively from the optimistic premise "there's got to be a cause up there somewhere." And of course there always is – once you know the terrestrial effect.

4 Empirical Tests? Vettius Valens and Six Men in a Boat

You will remember that four-fifths of our extant literary horoscopes come from a single source, the *Anthologies* of Vettius Valens. Although respected in antiquity – but not in his lifetime – Valens has garnered few bouquets from modern scholars.[5] So allow me to pay him the following compliment: among ancient astrologers he was the preeminent *empiricist*. Before you burst into laughter at the apparent oxymoron, remember that the empirical method *systematically* tests effects against *postulated* causes. Finding the *actual* causal mechanism comes later. First one must devise tests to see whether a particular effect, for example a certain type of violent death, does indeed regularly correlate with a postulated cause, for example a certain celestial configuration common to all or to an improbably high number of the horoscopes of those who did in fact die such deaths.

An astrologer who checks a horoscope after the event is not *ipso facto* an empiricist. Such an exercise is mere abductive rationalization ("it *must have been* this part of the configuration, not that part as we thought at the time"). Empiricism starts only when the possibility of disconfirmation is admitted, and that requires at a minimum two horoscopes and two lives lived. By modern standards it requires thousands. In order to isolate statistically significant correlations between certain professions (for example athletes) and certain configurations at birth (in this instance Mars in the ascendant or midheaven), Michel and Françoise Gauquelin compiled a database of some 25,000 horoscopes (Culver and Ianna 1977: 161–3). Vettius Valens' entire work contains 121 (Pingree 1986: xviii–xx).

For the would-be empiricist genethlialogy poses further problems that catarchic astrology does not. Catarchic astrology starts with a single (desired) outcome and searches for the auspicious moment based on a present or near future configuration of the heavens. Genethlialogy seeks to predict outcomes over an entire life span from the state of the

101

heavens at a given moment, the moment of birth (or conception). *When* something will happen (or is likely to happen) is as important as *what* will happen. Consequently the art of genethlialogy is greatly interested in the *stages* of a life, which planet will rule which period and when critical moments and changes of fortune are to be anticipated. In Book 5 (chapter 6, ed. Pingree)[6] for example, Valens investigates changes of fortune consequent on the "handing over" (*paradosis*) of rulership from planet to planet based on thirteen horoscopes dating from 102 to 153 CE (N&VH p. 101).

The most interesting and ambitious of Valens' "empirical" tests is found in the last chapter (6, ed. Pingree) of Book 7. With reluctance I have put weasel quotes around the word "empirical," for it will be all too apparent that the test is full of absurdities, including much arbitrary numerology. Nevertheless, I think it important to acknowledge those who took the baby steps in scientific methodology, not just those who made the adult strides.

The chapter in question contains eighteen horoscopes of which I shall single out a group of six. The six natives shared a common experience: they were involved in a near shipwreck and a chase by pirates. Was there a common factor in their horoscopes which indicated a crisis in the same year, even though they were born in different years and in different places? Notice that the question does not concern the qualitative specifics of the near disaster or even whether the natives were destined to undergo it together. That they did in fact share the experience merely establishes *a fortiori* that each of them underwent a crisis in the same year, which happened to be 154 CE. So what Valens needs to "discover" in the horoscopes is not a shared configuration which might suggest *qualitatively* similar crises (for example the malefics Saturn and Mars in, or in a sinister aspect to, a watery sign, which might be said to indicate danger at sea from shipwreck and pirates) but rather a *quantitative* factor which will bring the natives to crisis in the same year. In sum, Valens must find within the horoscopes an algorithm which in all six will yield a number N such that

$$\text{date of birth} + N = \text{date of crisis (154CE)}$$

N of course is the *age* of the native. But since a person whom we would call, for example, a "nineteen-year-old" would be said by the Greeks to be "in the twentieth year,"

$$N \text{ in context} = \text{age (in our sense)} + 1$$

In table 7.1 I have displayed the six horoscopes in columns in chronological order. N, the ordinal numeral for the native's age, is shown in the final line. N added to the year of birth (in the N&VH number) totals either 154 or 155. Working from the actual dates of birth, one finds that the crisis occurred no earlier than late May 154 CE (when L118 was in the middle of his 36th year) and no later than July 17 of the same year (when L127 reaches the end of his 27th year).

How then is N derived from the horoscopic data? Or from Valens' point of view, what is the algorithm built into the configurations of the heavens at the births of these six men which brings them ineluctably to a simultaneous crisis?

In fact Valens is not testing a hypothesis of his own but rather one which he attributes to a compendious late Hellenistic source passing under the name of the Egyptian pharaoh Nechepso (often called simply "the king") and his priest Petosiris, revered by many ancient astrologers as the founding fathers of their art. Vettius' purpose is not really to confirm, still less to disconfirm, his illustrious predecessors' hypothesis. It is his method, not his attitude, which foreshadows empiricism.

The hypothesis that Valens tests proposes

that the number of years to a crisis (N) is always a function of the "periods" (P) of the planets and/or of the "rising times" (RT) of the signs in which the planets are located.

What then are the "periods" and "rising times"? The "periods" are constants; each planet has one and one only: they are listed in the second column of the table. Although they are based on actual planetary periods

103

Table 7.1 The horoscopes of six men involved together in a crisis at sea (Vettius Valens, *Anthologies* 7.6)

N&VH no. Page/line (Pingree)	"Period"	L114.VII 274.14–21	L118 (3rd of 4 versions) 274.30–275.2	L120.II (4th of 4 versions) 274.22–28
Sun	19	Leo	Sag. P19, RT35.5	Aquarius
Moon	25	Libra P25, RT40	Libra	Scorpio
Saturn	30	Aries P15,[1] RT20	Gemini RT27.5	Cancer P30,[2] RT32.5/27.5[3]
Jupiter	12	Taurus P12, RT22,[3] P8[4]	Virgo	Libra RT42.5
Mars	15	Virgo	Sagittarius	Virgo P15, P20[1]
Venus	8	Virgo	Sagittarius P8	Capricorn P8, RT27
Mercury	20	Leo	Capricorn[1]	Aquarius
Horoscopos		Capr. RT28, P30[2]	Capricorn	Virgo
Clima		2	6	7
N (age at crisis)		in 40th year	middle of 36th year	in 35th year

L114.VII. (1) N = P 25 (Moon) + 15 (Mars)[1] = 40. (2) N = RT 40 (Libra) + 20 (Aries) = 60 × 2/3 = 40. "Therefore the crisis was double" (i.e. shipwreck *and* pirates). (3) N = RT 28 (Capr.) + P 12 (Jup. in trine to H) = 40. (4) N = P30 (Saturn)[2] + RT 22 (Taurus)[3] + P8 (Venus)[4] = 60 × 2/3 = 40.

[1]The period of Mars is assigned to Aries, not to Virgo where Mars was then located; the (unstated) warrant for this is that Aries is one of the houses of Mars. [2]The horoscopos does not have a period; Saturn's period is selected because Capricorn is one of his houses. [3]But only in clima 5, well to

the north. [4]The period of Venus is assigned to Taurus, not to Virgo where Venus was then located; the (unstated) warrant for this is that Taurus is one of the houses of Venus.

L118. (1) N = RT 27.5 (Gem.) + P 8 (Venus) = 35.5. (2) N = P 19 (Sun) + RT 35.5 (Sag.) = 54.5 × 2/3 = 36.3. At the end of this horoscope Valens adds, "here too the benefics [i.e. Venus and the Sun] participated."

[1]In the other three occurrences of this horoscope Mercury is (correctly) positioned in Scorpio.

L120.II. (1) N = P 15 (Mars: "the period of Mars was operative") + P 20 (Mercury)[1] = 35. (2) N = P 8 (Venus) + RT 27 (Capr.) = 35. (3) N = P 30 (Saturn)[2] + RT 32.5 (Cancer)[3] + P8 (Venus) = 70.5 × 1/2 = 35.25. (4) N = "And besides Jupiter [in Libra] and Saturn [in Cancer] shared the time [i.e. N]: RT 42.5 (Libra) + RT 27.5 (Cancer)[3] = 70 × 1/2 = 35.

[1]The period of Mercury is assigned to Virgo, not to Aquarius where Mercury was then located; the (unstated) warrant for this is that Virgo is one of the houses of Mercury. [2]Literally "the opposition of Saturn", i.e. the period of Saturn which is in Cancer, thus opposite Capricorn. [3]Different values for the rising time of Cancer are given in the third and fourth calculations.

Table 7.1 (cont.) The horoscopes of six men involved together in a crisis at sea (Vettius Valens, *Anthologies* 7.6)

N&VH no. Page/line (Pingree)	"Period"	L122.I.30 275.9–13	L127.VII 275.3–8	L133 275.14–18
Sun	19	Aquarius P19	Cancer P19, RT31.67	Taurus
Moon	25	Libra P25, P8[1]	Aries	Taurus P25
Saturn	30	Leo P30	Libra P8,[1] P30	Sagittarius
Jupiter	12	Sagittarius RT33	Gemini RT28.3, P12	Scorpio RT 33
				(*Continued*)

Table 7.1 (Continued)

N&VH no.		L122.I.30	L127.VII	L133
Page/line (Pingree)		275.9–13	275.3–8	275.14–18
	"Period"			
Mars	15	Libra	Leo P19[1]	Leo P19[1]
Venus	8	Capricorn	Cancer	Taurus P8
Mercury	20	Capricorn	Cancer	Taurus
Horoscopos		Pisces	Gemini	Pisces
Clima		6	1	2
N (age at crisis)		in 33rd year	in 27th year	in 22nd year

L122.I.30. (1) N = P 25 (Moon) + P 8[1] (Venus)= 33. (2) N = P 30 (Saturn) + P 19 (Sun) = 49 × 2/3 = 32.67. (3) N = RT 33 ("also the rising time of Sagittarius was operative because Jupiter was located there").

[1] The period of Venus is assigned to Libra, not to Capricorn where Venus was then located; the (unstated) warrant for this is that Libra is one of the houses of Venus.

L127.VII. (1) N = P 19 (Sun) + (Venus) 8[1] = 27. (2) N = RT 28.3 (Gem.) + P 12 (Jup.) = 40.3 × 2/3 = "close to" 27. (3) N = P 19 (Sun)[2] + RT 31.67 (Cancer) + P 30 (Saturn) = 80.67 × 1/3 = "close to" 27.

[1] The period of Venus is assigned to Libra, not to Cancer where Venus was then located; the (unstated) warrant for this is that Libra is one of the houses of Venus. [2] The period of the Sun is assigned to Leo, not to Cancer where the Sun was then located; the (unstated) warrant for this is that Leo is the house of the Sun.

L133. (1) N = P 19 (Sun)[1] + 25 (Moon) = 44 × 1/2 = 22. (2) RT 36 (Scorpio) + P8 (Venus) = 44 × 1/2 = 22.

[1] The period of the Sun is assigned to Leo, not to Taurus where the Sun was then located; the (unstated) warrant for this is that Leo is the house of the Sun.

106

(the sidereal period of Saturn is roughly thirty years, of Jupiter twelve years) or on elements of notable period relationships (the Sun's nineteen in the so-called Metonic cycle: 19 solar years = 235 lunar months), as a set they are astronomically meaningless. "Rising times," in contrast, are astronomically meaningful. The "rising time" of a sign of the zodiac is the number of degrees of the celestial equator which rise (in the literal sense of emerging above the eastern horizon) concurrently with the sign in question. Rising times differ depending on geographic latitude. Hence in each horoscope Valens gives the ancient equivalent of latitude, that is the *clima* (shown here in the penultimate line of the table).[7]

In taking rising times into consideration Valens is doing what any good experimentalist would do. He is factoring in a variable, namely place of birth. His algorithm is valid, he claims, *wherever* as well as whenever you were born. In practice Valens is neither consistent nor accurate in his values for RT.[8] Historically, however, the principles on which he constructs his experiment are of greater interest and importance than the procedural flaws.

As you will see from the table, the algorithm is quite undemanding in that N can be reached through many different combinations of P and/or RT and one also has the option of reaching it by multiplying a preliminary total by fractions of one-half, one-third, or two-thirds. Indeed, one begins to suspect that the algorithm is so lax that the required N could be reached one way or another in the horoscope of any and every native who did in fact undergo a crisis in the year 154 CE.

If N can be discerned one way or another in any horoscope after the event, imagine the difficulty of discerning it in a horoscope before the event and so predicting the age at which your client must anticipate a crisis. Which combination of periods and rising times do you select? My suspicion is that by judicious selection of permissible values for P and RT you could predict a crisis for any year in your client's life from the time of the consultation onwards – or "prove" that your client had already undergone a crisis in any year before.

In other words, even if tested indefinitely, Valens' hypothesis would seldom, if ever, be disconfirmed. But that would not verify the hypothesis, for one could never establish that the high correlation between the timing of life crises on the one hand and the planetary periods and rising times on the other was anything but an artifact of the generosity of the algorithm in allowing so many different values for P and RT in calculating N.

In fairness to Valens, we must return the exercise with its six horoscopes to its proper context in the *Anthologies* and concede that he is at some pains in other chapters to limit the options for P and RT. For example, in 4.11, a chapter "on the operative (*chrêmatistikou*) year," explains the criteria for selecting the proper planets for values of P and the proper signs for values of RT.[9] He uses L120.II (second version in N&VH = 4.11.165.1–10 Pingree) as an example; likewise L118 (second version in N&VH = 7.3.256.16–24 Pingree) in 7.3, a chapter "on the distribution of times." Essentially, Valens sees his task as determining, for a given situation or problem, which planet is active in which sign and why. "Whichever yields the required N" is not the answer, at least not explicitly.

5 Multiple Outcomes: Two of Valens' Six

Determining the inevitability of a crisis in 154 CE was not the only use that Valens made of the horoscopes of his six voyagers. Two of them in particular, L118 and L120.II, Valens used in other contexts. Methodologically this is as it should be. One would expect a certain degree of recurrence in the analyses of a would-be empirical astrologer, and one would be rightly suspicious if a whole new data set was brought to bear for each new problem. After all, if astrology is valid, the inquirer should be able to recycle successfully any horoscope through any inquiry into any type of outcome which the native did in fact undergo: the result should always (or at least generally) be a positive correlation between the outcome and the celestial configuration postulated for that type of outcome.

Consequently, L118 (first version) also appears among the horoscopes in a sign by sign discussion of various injuries and ailments (2.37): the native was bald and his penis was injured because "the ruler of Scorpio (Mars) was in Sagittarius" (106.26–7). He also suffered an eye injury, for Valens continues, "but Jupiter, the ruler of Mars and of the Daimon (?),[10] being found in the place of the god (place no. 9), made him see again through the god; and he became a soothsayer" (106.27–9). The eye injury, we learn in 7.3, a chapter on the "distribution of times," was but part of a larger crisis which the native underwent in his nineteenth year and which included the loss of his father to death by violence and a dangerous sea voyage. The voyage and the perils cannot be the same he experienced in 154 in the middle of his thirty-sixth year, for we are explicitly told here in 7.3 that the crisis occurred in his nineteenth year. Actually, the same algorithm is used in 7.3 as later in 7.6, only without the option of fractions: a number N is deduced from the relevant planetary periods and/or the rising times of the relevant signs. In 7.3, however, Valens concentrates less on the calculation of N, and more on the question of which planets are dominant for good or ill at the time of the crisis and so may be said to cause it. The problem is complicated by a partial reversal of fortune from bad to good in the following year. The question then is why does bad fortune prevail when $N = 19$ and mixed fortune when $N = 20$? Here is the solution (256.16–24, first in Valens' words and then in an explanatory paraphrase: note that the planetary positions given are always those at birth, not at the time of crisis):

1. "The Sun's period was operative." $N = P$ (Sun) $= 19$.
2. "Mars was with him and Saturn in opposition." Mars, in the same sign (Sagittarius) as the Sun, casts a sinister light over events of the nineteenth year; so does Saturn in opposition (in Gemini); for Mars and Saturn are malefics and opposition is a bad aspect.
3. "In the twentieth year, through an oracle of the god, he saw again." $N = 20$. The native's fortunes change for the better.
4. "Saturn was then operative, Gemini providing the twenty." Saturn was in Gemini. Gemini is one of the houses of Mercury. Mercury's period is twenty. Thus, $N = P$ (Mercury) $= 20$.
5. "Hence he suffered many misfortunes." Presumably, the malefic Saturn is the culprit.

109

6.   "Virgo too indicated twenty, Jupiter being in it. (The period) of
     Jupiter is twelve and of Venus, in quartile aspect, eight. The sum is
     twenty." N = P12 (Jupiter) + P8 (Venus) = 20. Jupiter and Venus
     are benefics and so bring good fortune in the twentieth year to
     modify the bad fortune brought by Saturn.

Like his slightly older shipmate, the native of L120.II was also predeceased
by a parent. We know this from the illustrative use of his horoscope in a
chapter (2.31) specifically devoted to that topic. Otherwise, although the
horoscope figures in a number of other chapters throughout the *Anthologies*, we learn no further details of the native's biography. So let us take as
our final example of Valens' after-the-fact interpretations his discussion of
why the native had to be predeceased by his mother rather than his father
(96.30–7). Here is the text, first with minimal supplements in parentheses
to render it more or less comprehensible. I make no apologies for serving it
up raw, as it were. It is the best I can offer by way of an unmediated glimpse
at the desk of a working astrologer as he earnestly toils to match the real
horoscopes of real people with the real outcomes of their lives some
eighteen-and-a-half centuries ago. It has been suggested (Pingree 1986:
v) that the native of L120.II was none other than Valens himself, which
would add a certain pathos to the exercise. It would also mean that Valens
was one of our "six men in a boat." I have delayed mentioning this
possibility out of respect for Valens' stance of anonymity. If he chose to
treat the native's identity as irrelevant, then so should we.

> Count (the days) from the rising of Sirius up to the date of birth.[11] Subtract
> twelves, and count off the remainder one by one within the twelve (signs)
> from (the sign of) the Moon. If (the count-off) ends in a male sign the
> father will predecease; if in a female sign, the mother. As in the present
> horoscope. Date of birth Mekhir 13; from Epiphi 25 to (Mekhir) 13 totals
> 203 (days). I subtracted sixteen twelves. Remainder eleven. (Counting off)
> the eleven from the Moon in Scorpio ended in Virgo, a female sign. Mars
> happened to be there too.[12] The predecease was the mother's.

Here is a paraphrase of sorts, which should make the actual procedure
and its internal logic clearer:

The assumed date for the rising of Sirius is Epiphi 25 = July 19. The native was born the following year on Mekhir 13 = February 8. Thus the interval is 203 days. Valens divides this number by twelve. The remainder is eleven. Valens then counts forward eleven *signs*, starting from and including the sign in which the Moon was located at birth.[13] That sign was Scorpio. Virgo is eleven signs on from Scorpio, counting inclusively. Virgo is a female sign. Therefore it was the native's mother who predeceased him, not his father.

Although Valens gives several alternative procedures for determining whether the mother or the father will be the predeceasing parent, L120.II is the only illustrative horoscope in the chapter (2.31). We are firmly back in the world of abductive reasoning, deduction from a postulated cause (the count ended in a female sign, didn't it?) with no attempt at confirmation from the horoscopes of other natives with a predeceased parent.

A final comment on the question itself. The procedure seems on the face of it to imply something which is manifestly untrue: that everyone is predeceased by one or other of their parents, and the only question is which – mother or father? But many people are predeceased by both parents and many by neither (one thinks of young soldiers dying in battle and, in pre-modern times, young women in childbirth). There seems then to be a concealed condition: *if* I am predeceased by a parent, which one will it be? And that is a very strange question to ask in practice. The topic, I suggest, is purely a record-based astrologer's exercise: what factor or index can I discern in the horoscopes of natives who have actually lost one or other parent to tell me why it had to be the father in some cases and the mother in others?

6 N&VH no. L621: The Horoscope of Islam

Fast-forward five hundred years from Valens to the horoscope of Islam and another century-and-a-half to the date of its actual composition in 775 CE. Neugebauer and Van Hoesen consider it the last of the Greek horoscopes, arguing that it is somewhat too early to be considered a

111

product of the return of astrology to Byzantium from the Arab world. Although chronologically an outlier, L621 is undoubtedly the best example of after-the-fact horoscopal interpretation on a grand scale. Indeed I know of nothing else comparable from antiquity. So let us see how a century-and-a-half of actual history and a further half-century of history foreseen can lie coiled like a spring in the configuration of the heavens at a single moment of time.

The horoscope is displayed in diagrammatic form in figure 7.2. The data and the operative relationships shown are taken directly from the text (N&VH pp. 158–60; Usener 1965: 273–5).

Earlier in this chapter (section 2) we sketched out the imagined casting of the horoscope at 9:00 a.m. on September 1, 621, and its principal import, the spectacular rise of the new nation and its rapid conquest of the entire Near East. The date and time of the horoscope, we saw, was the actual moment when the merchant from Arabia

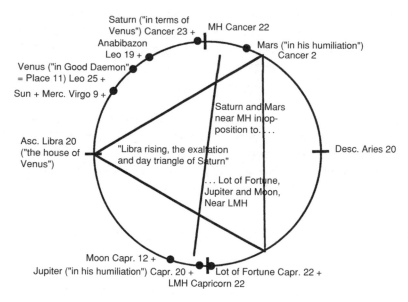

Figure 7.2 The horoscope of Islam, 9:00 a.m., September 1, 621 CE, Constantinople(?) (N&VH no. L621)

imparted the news about the new prophet to the astrologer "Stephanus." The occasion, we also noted, was a fiction invented by the actual author a century-and-a-half later to give the horoscope an aura of immediacy and authenticity. Even so, it is a strange choice for a *katarche* or "beginning." For nations one usually selects an inaugural event, such as the signing of the Declaration of Independence for the United States of America. Islam's inaugural event is the *hijra*, Muhammad's move from Mecca to Medina on July 16, 622. It was an extraordinary piece of Eurocentrism to predate the *katarche* to the beginning of the official Byzantine year more than ten months earlier.[14]

The date then is explicable, if not excusable. What of the time of day, "the third hour" or about 9:00 a.m.? Time of day is crucial, because only if one knows it can one determine which sign was at the ascendant, at the midheaven, and so on; also crucial is the precise location of the planets with reference to the centers and places. And a mere couple of hours makes a world of difference: literally, it makes a different world.

Our story tells how Stephanus immediately took measurements with his astrolabe and determined from the longitude of the Sun (Virgo 9° 5′) that the twentieth degree of Libra was rising and the twenty-second degree of Cancer culminating. Let us reverse the story. For some reason our author wants Libra rising: accordingly he fixes the time of the consultation at the third hour from sunrise. Why Libra? Because, as he tells us, Islam "will immediately assault and lord it over many nations, for *Zygos* (Libra) rising brings slavery to all men." How so? The prognosis rests on an etymological word play: Greek *zygon/zygos* means "yoke"; therefore *Zygos* rising indicates imposition of the "yoke of oppression."[15]

Immediately after he has given the longitudes of the Sun and the four cardinal points on the fixed circle of places, Stephanus bursts out, "Oh the misery! alas the change of things." Clearly the horoscope is bad news – for everyone, that is, except the nation now coming to birth. Other than Libra rising, with subjugation as its intent, what is so "dis-astr-ous" about the configuration? In fifty lines of text Stephanus goes on to explain. What follows is the first set of factors operative in the horoscope, constituting its "premise" (*protasis*). In form I present it as a loose paraphrase with some commentary and some reordering.

113

1. As already noted, Libra rising indicates subugation (*by* rather than *of* the new nation).
2. Libra is the exaltation of Saturn and in the "daytime triangle" of Saturn. This means that we should pay particular attention to Saturn, who is active and powerful in the horoscope. Saturn is also a malefic, a notorious celestial "evil-doer." Remember that the horoscope adopts the Byzantine point of view: what's bad for us is good for them.
3. Saturn is also very close to the midheaven, which further enhances his power.
4. The other particularly active and powerful planet is Venus, for she is approaching the zenith, she is currently in one of the more auspicious of the twelve places (no. 11: "Good Daemon") along with the ascending node of the lunar orbit (Anabibazon: see above, chapter 6, note 19), she is in Leo, and she is the householder of the rising sign, Libra. As a benefic, Venus is good for them, and therefore bad for us, their enemies.
5. Celestial bodies when they culminate at midheaven are *ipso facto* due south on the meridian. Saturn is thus almost due south and Venus is approaching it (she will be there somewhat over two hours later).

Consequently, we have to do with a southern people (Arabia is indeed south from Byzantium), under the patronage of Saturn and Venus. "The horoscopal premise (*protasis*) indicates a nation of Saturn's condition and Venus' polity" (273.19–21), destined to sweep all before it: as already quoted (above, section 2) "... outstanding in great strength and unrestrained speed and constant motion and of enduring possession, with epic battles and most brilliant deeds of valor and distinguished by a new type of state" (N&VH trans.).

Stephanus has chosen to deduce Islam's planetary patrons from the configuration of the horoscope. There was another way open to him, and that was to consult the chapters on chorography in the manuals. There you will find lists of the signs of the zodiac governing each region and country; likewise the planets, often in pairs. Chorography was the ultimate in ethnic stereotyping. Like most things astrological, chorography offers plenty of alternatives: you can usually find the signs or planets you want hovering over the target country. Stephanus could, for example, have gone to Ptolemy's *Tetrabiblos* (2.3.64) and found that Saturn and Venus do indeed rule the south-east quadrant of the known world. However, he would also have found that within that quadrant a group of countries in the north-west quarter, including Arabia, have as their co-rulers Jupiter, Mars, and Mercury (2.3.65–6). In particular, the homeland of Islam, then known for its prosperity (especially in the spice trade) as Arabia Felix ("Fortunate Arabia"), is assigned to Sagittarius and Jupiter (2.3.66). They are graceful people with an open society.

The geo-political realities of Ptolemy's day endured more or less up to the Islamic conquests in the seventh century, at least in the Levant. Stephanus in the eighth knew a radically different world, in which what was left of the empire of the Romans (the *Rômaioi*) confronted Islam and the Arabs where Anatolia ended and Syria began. His "new type of state" was the Ummayad Caliphate centered on luxurious Damascus, and it is clearly that society that he has in mind when he describes the characteristics of those co-ruled by Saturn and Venus. Indeed, he may be drawing directly or indirectly on Ptolemy when he contrasts a certain "effeminacy" and "softness" of bodily manner and self-presentation, notably in dress, with this people's "courage" and "manliness" of soul (Usener 274.15–16, cf. *Tetr.* 2.3.65).[16] The lesson to be drawn? Do not underestimate these Saturn–Venus types: appearances are deceptive. One final link with Venus, available to Stephanus but not to his astrological predecessors: Friday is the Muslim day of prayer and Friday is the day of Venus (274.13–14).

Looking back over the nightmare (from the Byzantine point of view) of the preceding century-and-a-half, Stephanus wants to know why this new nation with its new religion, from an obscure part of the world not previously noted for its military resources, had been able to rob the eastern Roman empire of a good half of its territories and utterly overwhelm the equally well-endowed Persian empire. Why had one of those two world powers survived, albeit diminished, while the other had not? And when, oh when, would the tide turn?

To continue with our paraphrase of the horoscope's operative factors:

6. Nations under Jupiter are in serious trouble, for Jupiter is both in his humiliation (Capricorn) and close to the nadir at lower midheaven. This factor explains the annihilation of the Persian empire.
7. Nations under the Moon are in trouble for the same reason.
8. Mars foreshadows mixed fortune. He is in his humiliation, which is bad news for the nations under him, but he is also close to midheaven, which is good news. The outcome will be set-backs but survival. This will apply to the kingdoms of the Romans (i.e. the eastern empire), the Khazars, the Turks, and the Bulgars.
9. Mercury's effect is not explained.[17] But since those he governs are among the losers, it is presumably malefic. The losers include Egypt and Libya (under Mercury and Mars respectively) and Palestine and Syria (Moon and Mercury).
10. Crucial is the Sun, under whom stands Rome. Rome "will be exempt from the yoke of such a nation" (274.4–5). Why the Sun is effective in the horoscope is not explained (though see below).
11. A summary at this point (275.9–14) emphasizes the aspect of opposition which obtains between the lot of fortune, Jupiter, and the Moon at lower midheaven and Saturn and Mars at midheaven (see figure 7.1). "Because of this all the nation's good fortune will depend on the sword, and it will have plenty of strength to subject (others)."

Islam's future, as Stephanus sees it, is not governed solely by factors built into the celestial configurations at 9:00 a.m. on September 1, 621. As time rolls on, the circling of the planets brings ever-changing new configurations into play. Imagine the zodiac circle of figure 7.2 extended into a new dimension upwards from the surface of the page. Up and around the lengthening cylinder so formed spiral the planets in complex but entirely predictable figures. One spiral of the Sun we call a year. The spiral that interests Stephanus is naturally that of Islam's planetary patron, Saturn. Stephanus "predicts" an entire history of Islam with twenty-four rulers, Muhammad and the caliphs who succeeded him, lasting for six thirty-year Saturn cycles plus the twenty or so years it would take for Saturn to run part of the seventh from Cancer 23°+ to the beginning of Aries. When Stephanus made his predictions nineteen of the twenty-four rulers were already history, so he could "predict" with some confidence their looks, their characters, their deeds, and their deaths. Deaths are dated, and sometimes explained, by the movement of Saturn from sign to sign.

The duration of Islam's rule and the astrological causes of its demise are determined in two widely separated places (275.24–276.13 and 286.18–287.5). The first calculation, made by a procedure too lengthy and complicated to replicate here, yields 152 years of domination. The difficulty with this sum is that Islam's time should have run out in 773 CE, which is two years *before* the date of the horoscope's composition based on the historical facts which Stephanus appears to know. It may then be that Stephanus *recalibrated* the horoscope, firstly by adding the caliph list or extending it to a date still well in the future, and secondly by making the end of Islam's dominion coincide the death of the twenty-fourth caliph. The superseded date and the method for calculating it were nevertheless left in the text: a catastrophe which did not happen can always be explained as a crisis survived.

The twenty-four caliphs will rule for about two hundred years in all, which sets the new expiry date at around 821 CE. The problem with the second procedure for determining the date astrologically is that the text is seriously corrupt and lacunose in the relevant passage. However, one can say with certainty first that the procedure is not based on the configurations in the original horoscope but on the configurations which *will* obtain when the end is reached. To return to our metaphor, the two-dimensional disk of the horoscope has been extended into a three-dimensional cylinder two hundred years long. There at the cross-section the astrologer, who is actually standing at about the three-quarter point, reads disaster in the configurations of the terminal disk.

What goes wrong at the two-hundred-year point? Though the specifics are confused, it is clear that the planets supporting Islam will run into trouble and be diminished while those supporting Rome will be strengthened. On "their" team, Saturn will be in Aries, his humiliation, and Venus will be "hidden," in other words too close to the Sun to be visible either as a morning star or as an evening star. On "our" team, Mars will be in Capricorn, his exaltation, and (for reasons which it is impossible to reconstruct from the text as it stands) the Sun will again be dominant. These conditions will be met for the three planets proper early in 822 CE, a fact which an astrologer could easily have foretold in 775. "And the kingdom of the Romans will rule because of the return (*apokatastasis*) of the Sun" (287.4–5).

The primacy of the Sun and his partisanship in the interests of the Byzantine cause are simple givens in the horoscope, so obvious to Stephanus and his immediate readers that they do not need to be made explicit. Why should the Sun favor the Romans? If one seeks an answer in chorography, one should look back to old Rome, the former seat of empire in the west. In Ptolemy's system, Italy in its entirety is related to the Sun, causing its inhabitants to be "hegemonic, philan-thropic, and public-spirited" (*Tetr.* 2.3.62). There are, though, deeper sub-texts. On the eve of the Roman empire's Christianization the Sun, as "companion" of its emperor and the "unconquered" guarantor of its hegemony, was as close to being its common god as was possible in so polytheistic a society. Christ, the "Sun of Righteousness," simply took over the reins of the solar chariot. Lastly, while it needs to be pointed out that Muslims are Friday people, it goes without saying that we in Constantinople are Sunday people.

Astrology is an intensely conservative art. More than four centuries after the Christening of the empire a Christian astrologer could still speak of the empire's planetary gods wresting power back from the planetary gods favoring Islam.

8

A Matter of Life and Death: "Starters," "Destroyers," and "Length of Life." Some Sociopolitical Implications of Astrology

1 Dangerous Territory

"...all very interesting, no doubt. But can you tell me when my rich and childless uncle will, like, pass on? And while you're at it, can you tell me who'll be the next emperor?" It is not in the interests of public order in general, or in the interests of your uncle and the current emperor in particular, that you as a professional astrologer be able to answer these questions – or even that you be *thought* able to answer them. It was precisely because, even in the face of a considerable and robust skepticism, astrologers were widely believed to have those abilities that the practice of astrology was a law-and-order issue in Rome and the empire.

At the end of this chapter we shall look at the actual legislation passed against astrologers, at their periodic expulsions from Rome, and at the

119

stories, both historical and fictional, generated by what one might these days call "extreme genethlialogy." First, though, we must look at the theory.

2 The "Starter," the "Destroyer," and the "Length of Life"

Given the illegality of requesting or giving an astrological consultation about length of life or date of death, one might expect the manuals to be entirely silent on the topic. On the contrary, there are few topics on which the manuals are more garrulous. Apparently, the theoreticians of astrology at least were not afraid to speculate about the celestial indicators of life and death or, if their interests took them that way, to analyze the horoscopes of the dead to determine why people had to die when they did and what configurations in their horoscopes brought them to their ends.

As usual, there was always a fail-safe. Sufficient ambiguities and complexities were built into the system as a whole, as also into the systems of individual experts, so as to render the manuals useless as practical tools for determining death dates in advance. And that is as it should be. "Of course your uncle's death date is encoded in his horoscope, but why would you think I could possibly decipher it before the unhappy event?"

Theoretically length of life could be calculated in one or other (or both) of two ways: either cumulatively by adding the number of years assigned to successive life stages by the planets and signs through the "periods" and rising times which we encountered in the last chapter; or by determining a starting point and an end point at different places on the natal chart and (in the simplest form) by measuring the arc of longitude in between, counting each degree as a year of life.[1] I shall concentrate on the second procedure.

Astrology likes causal agents and so, as well as a starting point and an end point, a birth-star and a death-star must be identified; a "starter" (*aphetês*) and a "destroyer" (*anairetês*) as they were termed. The starter, in Bouché-Leclerq's metaphor (1899: 411), throws the little ball of your life onto the roulette of the zodiac at the launching point (*aphetikos topos*), and the destroyer stops it dead in its tracks at the point of destruction (*anairetikos topos*).

Since obfuscation under the guise of clarification is the theoretician's aim,[2] it would be best, as in the last chapter, to illustrate the procedure from a post-mortem horoscope, with the proviso that the method there used is but one of an innumerable set of variants. By a pleasing coincidence, the most suitable horoscope for our present purpose is the first and earliest literary horoscope in the Neugebauer and Van Hoesen collection. You will recall that the horoscope of Islam, with which we ended the preceding chapter, is the last and latest.

3 An Example: N&VH no. L–71

No. L–71 (72 BCE) is embedded together with no. L–42 (43 BCE) in a chapter from the work of Ti. Claudius Balbillus on the "method for (determining) life spans from the starter and destroyer" preserved in two much later sources. What follows here is a translation of the text in *CCAG* 8.4 (236.24–237.10) in numbered paragraphs with explanations in parentheses.[3] The speaker ("I") is the excerptor; "he" is Balbillus. I have presented the horoscope diagrammatically in figure 8.1.

1. And again he says that for another theme the Moon was in Scorpio 4°, the Sun in Capricorn 22°, and Saturn in Capricorn 4°, and Jupiter in Virgo 14°, and Mars in Aquarius 14°, and Mercury in Aquarius 12°, and Venus in Pisces 25°, and the *horoscopos* in Gemini.
2. And since the luminaries (Sun and Moon) fell away from the centers (i.e. neither the Sun nor the Moon was in the signs occupying the *horoscopos*, midheaven, descendant, or lower midheaven), he went to the *epanaphoras* (i.e. the signs which follow the signs at the centers).
3. And he did not take the *horoscopos* as starter, or the Sun which was in the *epanaphora* to the descendant (i.e. the Sun was in Capricorn, the sign which follows Sagittarius into the descendant).

4. But he took Saturn in Capricorn as starter: this, I think, because Saturn had the greater claim (i.e. greater than the Sun, also in Capricorn) in the theme, being on his own throne (i.e. in his astrological house).

5. And he says that Mars in Aquarius is the destroyer.

6. And he computed the distance in degrees from Aries to Mars, and that total, he said, would be the number of years of (the native's) life.

As it stands, the sixth and final step is completely opaque to a modern reader. Why does Aries suddenly enter the picture? The reason and the logic behind it are as follows. If the life were to run clockwise round the zodiac from the starter to the destroyer, the length of the native's life

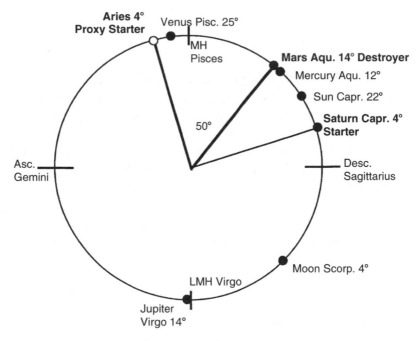

Clockwise arc from proxy Starter at Aries 4° to Destroyer at
Aquarius 14° = 50° = 50 years of life.

Figure 8.1   A horoscope of January 21, 72 BCE (N&VH no. L–71)

would be two-hundred-and-ninety years; if counterclockwise, seventy. The first number is impossible, but so is the second, for Balbillus knew not only when the native was born but also when he died and that his length of life was in fact fifty years. Accordingly, he reduced the first number by moving the starter to a proxy in quadrature three full quadrants away.[4] The proxy is thus at Aries 4°, and the arc from there clockwise to the destroyer (Mars at Aquarius 14°) totals fifty degrees and so yields the required fifty years.

Notice particularly the wide range of alternatives available to the practitioner at every stage. What or whom to choose as the starter and what or whom as the destroyer? Which way round the zodiac? How to adjust preliminary numbers? As length of life calculations go, L–71 is among the more straightforward, which is what one would expect in such an early horoscope. Post-mortem it all seems logical enough, since it is driving inexorably to the known solution of fifty year of life, but before...?

4 What Does an Imperial Horoscope Look Like? N&VH no. L76: The Horoscope of Hadrian

"If I remember correctly, you were also asking about the next emperor, no? Well don't go there either. You know very well – or you should know – that it's illegal, treason in fact, and you and I both could come to spectacularly nasty ends if it ever gets out that you've consulted me about it. In any case, as my colleague Firmicus Maternus points out in his excellent manual (*Mathesis* 2.30.5), it wouldn't work. The emperor, as a god, is above fate, so none of us can read his destiny in the stars. Consider yourself lucky that I'm not turning you in, because if I did, as Firmicus also says (2.30.7), I would then have your death on my conscience."[5]

Fortunately our curiosity these days is no longer bound by such constraints. What configurations in a horoscope, then, might confer imperial potential? As before, a good way of answering this is to look at an after-the-event analysis of an actual life lived, in this case that of an actual emperor.

N&VH no. L76 is the horoscope of the emperor Hadrian who was born at about 6:00 a.m. on January 24, 76 CE, and ruled from 117 to 138.[6] The horoscope was analyzed some time – we do not know even approximately how long – after Hadrian's death by one Antigonus of Nicaea. Antigonus' analyses of this and two other related horoscopes are preserved by the early fifth-century author Hephaestion of (Egyptian) Thebes in his *Apo-telesmatica* ("Outcomes"), 2.18.22–52 (1.157.28–162.30, ed. Pingree). I have presented Hadrian's horoscope diagrammatically in figure 8.2.

Antigonus addresses our question directly:

> This man became emperor (*autocratôr*) because (1) the two luminaries (Sun and Moon) were with the ascendant, and (2) especially because the Moon ... was in conjunction in the very same degree with the ascendant and with Jupiter (all three at Aquarius 1°), (3) who (i.e. Jupiter) was also

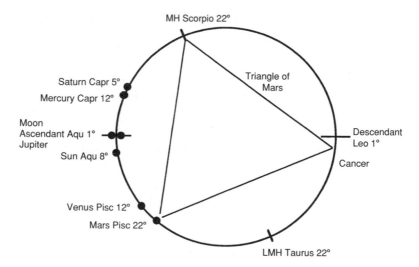

Figure 8.2 The horoscope of the emperor Hadrian, January 24, 76 CE (N&VH no. L76)

due to make his morning phase after seven days (i.e. his first visibility in the pre-dawn sky following his conjunction with the Sun). (4) And the Moon's attending planets (lit. "spear-carriers") were found in favorable positions: (a) Venus in her own exaltation (Pisces), (b) Mars in his own triangle and his own terms,[7] (c) both in . . . *epanaphora* with respect to the Moon (i.e. in the next sign to rise after the Moon's sign: Pisces follows Aquarius into the ascendant). (5) And besides, the cosmos-ruling (*kosmokratôr*) Sun was the Moon's attendant ("spear-carrier" again) . . . (6) And he himself (i.e. the Sun) was attended by Saturn in his own house (Capricorn) and by Mercury, both at their morning rising. (7) It is also significant that the Moon is about to come into conjunction with a certain bright fixed star at the twentieth degree (of Aquarius).

Are you any the wiser on the inevitability of Hadrian ascending the throne? No? Well, that is because the astrologer must work with what he's got, and here he is constrained on the one side by the actual horoscope – no astrologer can rearrange the stars – and on the other by the brute facts of history: Hadrian did actually become emperor. There really is no template for the ideal imperial horoscope. Some horoscopes, like Hadrian's, have a preponderance of positive configurations and some of negative – at least superficially. But a skilled astrologer can always make you a silk purse out of a sow's ear or, if you would rather lead a quiet life, a sow's ear out of a silk purse. It all depends on your ambitions and the ambitions of your parents, friends, and backers; also on the paranoia of the authorities: it was not unknown for rivals or potential rivals of the current emperor to be framed with rumors of an imperial horoscope and ambitions to match.

Two features of Hadrian's imperial horoscope are worth comment before moving on to the sociopolitical world of astrologers and their clients. Firstly, notice the elaborate metaphor of "attendance," literally "spear-carrying" (*doryphoria*). The stars, "dance attendance" on one another, and that dance replicates and so foreshadows a courtly pageant. In the heavens, at the moment of Hadrian's birth, the Moon rises and she is followed in succession by the Sun, Venus, and Mars acting as her spear-carriers. The Sun, who is the true "cosmocrat" as Hadrian will be "autocrat," rises next preceded by his own spear-carriers Saturn and

Mercury. No human eye witnessed – or could possibly have witnessed – the actual celestial pageant of that day, but an astrologer's imagination could and did.

Secondly, the puzzle of the identity of the "bright fixed star in the twentieth degree (of Aquarius)" – there is no bright fixed star in Aquarius – can be solved only by reference to other astrological literature, specifically Firmicus Maternus. At *Mathesis* 6.2 Firmicus says that although there are brilliant stars in all the signs, there are "royal" stars in only four: Leo, Scorpio, Aquarius, and Taurus. The "royal" in Aquarius he locates, just as Antigonus does, in the twentieth degree. If the full Moon is rising or culminating at the moment of birth, says Firmicus, the bright star in Aquarius, like Regulus in Leo, "decrees the insignia of royal power and imperial dignity" (6.2.3). In Hadrian's horoscope the Moon isn't full – she's a waning crescent so close to the Sun that her rising could not have been observed – but she is precisely at the ascendant.

So is the royal star in Aquarius just an astrological fiction, invented to complete a set of bright stars more or less in quadrature around the heavens, the three others being the very real Aldebaran in Taurus, Regulus in Leo, and Antares in Scorpio? If it was a fiction, it was certainly a very durable one. More likely, though, it should be identified with the actual star Formalhaut, the lucida of the Southern Fish, which *in longitude* is in Aquarius although in latitude it is well to the south.[8]

5 Astrologers in the Hot Seat – and Nervous Emperors

The story of astrology's hold on the imaginations of the Roman imperial elite – and through their imaginations on their politics and actions too – has been well told by others, notably by F. H. Cramer in his still indispensable *Astrology in Roman Law and Politics* (1954).[9] Here then I can be brief.

First the law and what we might term executive action. In 11 CE the emperor Augustus issued an edict in which "it was forbidden to diviners to prophesy to any person alone or to prophesy regarding death even if others should be present" (Cassius Dio 56.25.5, trans. Cramer). Hence Firmicus Maternus' advice to budding astrologers: "You will give your replies in public and with this caution beforehand to those about to make their enquiries, that you will speak in a clear voice, so that nothing be asked of you that it is illegal to ask or to answer" (*Mathesis* 2.30.3). The cases which we hear about mainly involve speculation about the emperor, current or future. In practice then the charge was lèse-majesté or treason. Periodically, both before and after Augustus' edict, astrologers were collectively expelled from Rome and Italy as a sort of public cleansing of the morally undesirable. These actions had been initiated under the republic by command of an appropriate magistrate, then under the empire by decree of the Senate and later by edict of the emperor (Cramer 1954: 233–81).

Ancient societies generally did not, and logistically could not, aspire to totalitarian control. So the astrological riff-raff drifted back and the well-connected never left. Just how well-connected and respectable astrologers could become is best illustrated by the father-and-son pair Tiberius Claudius Thrasyllus and Tiberius Claudius Balbillus, the latter of whom we have already met (above, section 3).[10] The father was the friend and astrological consultant to the emperor Tiberius (14–37 CE), the son the particular friend of Claudius (41–54) and the adviser of Nero (54–68) and Vespasian (69–79) at the start of his reign. Their names show them to be Greeks who acquired Roman citizenship. Balbillus reached equestrian rank and had an amazingly varied career in public service, including the posts of chief of engineers for Claudius' invasion of Britain, head of the Museum – in effect the university – and of the Library at Alexandria (his native city), and prefect of Egypt. Egypt was one of the most vital and sensitive provinces of the empire, and its governorship was accordingly reserved for persons of equestrian rank. Members of the noble senatorial class were not even allowed to enter the country without imperial permission.

The astrological advice of Thrasyllus, Balbillus, and their like was literally a matter of life and death. At the appearance of a comet Balbillus, it was said, advised Nero that a sinister omen of this type was customarily diverted from a ruler by judicious culling of the elite

(Suetonius, *Nero* 36.1). Balbillus may then have blood on his hands, though whether he should be held responsible for the subsequent crushing of the "conspiracy" which took out the philosopher Seneca and the poet Lucan it is hard to say. Probably Nero would have continued to purge the nobility as he did, advice or no advice, but Balbillus, at the least, confirmed Nero in his murderous course. Thrasyllus, as the stories go, exercised a more benign influence over his patron Tiberius, persuading him to postpone certain preemptive strikes against his supposed enemies on the grounds that the old emperor still had ten years ahead of him in which to act at his leisure (Cassius Dio 58.27.2–3; Suetonius, *Tiberius* 62.3). The story implies that the astrologer "knows" or is utterly convinced that he "knows" the looming death date predetermined by the stars. Thrasyllus himself was in an exquisitely precarious position. His granddaughter, Ennia Thrasylla, was married to the prefect of the praetorian guard, Naevius Sertorius Macro. At the same time she was carrying on an affair, possibly with her husband's connivance, with the front-runner for the succession, Caius Caligula. In the event, Thrasyllus predeceased Tiberius in 36 CE and so did not witness Caligula's accession to the throne the following year – or the destruction of his own granddaughter and Macro the year after that. Thrasyllus, like many another, is reported to have foretold his own death to the precise hour (Cassius Dio 58.27.2–3).

The tales of the astrologers in first-century CE imperial Rome should be taken with more than a pinch of salt.[11] Even for skeptical historians stories of an ineluctable fate, and more especially stories about those who *believe* that an ineluctable fate is bearing down upon them, are irresistible. Such stories add drama, structure, and motivation to the telling of history. Ultimately, though, the factuality or otherwise of particular stories is less important, at least to the social historian, than the flavor of the story-telling as a whole. For the social historian, especially when studying the mentality of a culture, "urban myths" are on a par with actual events. So by way of example let us look at a couple of stories from the last days of Domitian (assassinated in 96 CE) as related by Suetonius (*Domitian* 14–17).

As so often, the account of the crisis is preceded by the premonitions, which in retrospect seem unusually numerous and dire. Among these,

> what disturbed him most ... was a prediction by the astrologer Ascletarion, and its sequel. This man, when charged, made no secret of having revealed the future, which he had foreseen by magical means. Domitian at once asked whether he could prophesy the manner of his [Ascletarion's] end, and upon Ascletarion's replying that he would very soon be torn to pieces by dogs, had him executed on the spot, and gave orders for the funeral rites to be conducted with the greatest care, as a further proof that all magicians lied. But while the funeral was in progress a sudden gale scattered the pyre and a pack of stray dogs mangled the astrologer's half-burned corpse. Latinus, the comic actor, who happened to witness this incident, mentioned it at dinner when he brought Domitian the latest City gossip. (15.3, trans. Graves)

The story follows a standard pattern: fate is fixed, even down to minor details; the true professional "speaks truth to power," even when it's the truth of his own dreadful ending; power cannot alter that truth, try as it may.

More plausible is the story of Domitian's own death soon thereafter and the ruse by which he was lulled into a false sense of security. The day before, he is said to have prophesied melodramatically, "tomorrow the Moon will bloody itself in Aquarius, and a deed will be done of which men will speak throughout the world" (16.1). Now the Moon, as everyone then knew, moves quite rapidly from sign to sign, covering on average somewhat under half a sign every day. The Moon then would be in Aquarius for about fifty-three hours. The conspirators in effect put palace time forward, and when Domitian asked what hour it was he was told it was the sixth although it was actually the fifth. So Domitian let down his guard, thinking the Moon had now passed beyond Aquarius, and the conspirators struck. Again, it is not a question of where the Moon actually was but of where the parties *thought* she was. Then again the whole story may be a study-bound astrologer's fabrication, cooked up after the event from the calculated positions of the planets at the known hour of Domitian's death.[12] Just for the record, my Voyager II

129

program (see above, chapter 3, section 7) tells me that on September 18, 96 CE, the Moon left Aquarius between twelve midnight and 1:00 a.m. on September 19. However, if one follows the calibration of the zodiac, much used in astrology, which sets the equinoxes and solstices at the eighth degree rather than at the beginning of their signs, the Moon left Aquarius between 10:00 and 11:00 a.m. on the eighteenth, which was indeed the fifth hour of the day of Domitian's death. In that case, if Suetonius' account is veridical, Domitian, with or without professional help, was monitoring the lunation closely and accurately. Since the Moon was then nearing full, he would have been able to supplement figures derived from tables with observation on the prior evenings. If the story is fictional, then all one can say is that the astrologer who made it up was using accurate lunar tables calibrated to a vernal equinox at Aries 8°.

I want finally to return to Thrasyllus and Balbillus not as persons of power behind the throne but as astrologers. In a modern context I would say "professional astrologers." In 1954 it was still possible to speak, as Frederick Cramer does, of "gentlemen astrologers," which is nearer the mark. In fact they were amateurs in the old-fashioned sense of persons of means free to pursue an art with pretensions to liberality, however compromised by the vulgar activities of street astrologers. Both father and son were highly regarded intellectuals. Balbillus we have seen was head of the Museum and Library at Alexandria, arguably the empire's most prestigious scholarly appointment. Thrasyllus for his part was the leading expert of his time on Plato and Platonism (Tarrant 1993): his arrangement of the canon of Plato's works remains current today. Both wrote astrological treatises, only scraps of which survive.[13] Among the scraps from Balbillus is the earliest literary horoscope, N&VH no. L–71, which we looked at above (section 3). Now that we have viewed a little of Balbillus' and his father's careers, we can appreciate the irony that "length of life" was as a matter of fact Balbillus' astrological specialty.

From where did Balbillus obtain the two horoscopes L–71 and L–42? Balbillus was active in the middle of the first century CE and yet was in possession of the horoscope of someone born more than a century earlier in 72 BCE. While that horoscope cannot have been interpreted in respect of length of life before the native's death in 22 BCE (give or take a year), the astrological particulars or at the very least the day and hour of his or her birth would have been on record long before.

Interestingly, we are in a position to say what archives, in all probability, Balbillus had access to. A daughter of his, we know, married the heir to the throne of Commagene, a client kingdom of Rome's on the Parthian frontier north of Syria. Now the earliest of the "original" (non-literary) horoscopes in the N&VH collection is no. −61 (62 BCE). It happens to be the horoscope, in the form of a large sculpted relief, of a sacred site constructed on a mountain top in his realm by the then king of Commagene. The simplest answer to our initial question is that Balbillus acquired his astrological data from the archives of the astrologically oriented family into which he had married his daughter.[14]

9

Conclusion: Why Bother with Ancient Astrology in the Twenty-First Century?

The hold that astrology undoubtedly had on Graeco-Roman imperial society was a function of its *imagined* predictive power, not of its actual track record. Then as now, many believed that there was "something to it." Some fervently believed so and were highly and impressively articulate about their beliefs. Others were skeptical, and since the Greeks (and Romans immersed in Greek philosophical and literary culture, as those of the elite were) loved nothing better than a good argument, a vigorous debate about the validity and utility of astrology ensued.

I warned in my preface that we would have no space for that debate here, and indeed we don't. Its omission is tolerable, firstly because others have addressed it fully and well, and secondly because it has little abiding relevance, except of course as a minor chapter in the annals of ancient philosophy. While not in a formal sense disproving astrology – you cannot falsify what cannot be verified empirically – science since the seventeenth century has effectively rendered astrology less and less credible: firstly by removing earth from the center of the universe and more recently by removing a privileged center from the universe itself; and secondly by reuniting earth with heaven by subordinating both to the same physical laws, Newtonian or other. Gravity rules (or did), not astral "influence."

If ancient astrology was just another pseudo-predictive system, like divination from the entrails of sacrificial animals, why write a whole book about it, even a "brief" one? If we set aside astrology's interest as a not insignificant presence in the cultural landscape of antiquity, why indeed?

My answer is inherent in the emphasis I have placed on after-the-event analysis in the "literary" horoscopes, where lives lived are measured against the celestial configurations at birth. Astrology, I have suggested, furnished an idiom in which to tell stories endowed with certain patterns of meaning. These may be grand narratives, such as the destiny of Islam (N&VH L621: above, chapter 7, section 6), or petty narratives – one of my favorites being L483 "concerning a small lion, whether he will be tamed." The great majority were of course the stories of individual human lives. These stories, if we accept astrology's foundational premise that things in heaven foreshadow things on earth, exist as potentialities in the innumerable – but not infinite – configurations and relationships of the "nativity." Knowing the actual outcomes, the reflective astrologer can identify the operative configurations and relationships and so render the story accurately in "star-talk," as I have elsewhere characterized the language of astrology (Beck 2006: 153–89). "Operative" (*chrêmatistikos*) is a technical term in genethlialogy. The *operative* configurations and relationships are the *activated* circuits in the horoscope's wiring diagram. If astrology is a language, then the operative configurations and relationships are the phrases – let us say the "astremes" – selected from the horoscope for the story of the life lived.

That genethlialogy is a system of signs, more precisely a system for organizing and interpreting signs, no one would dispute. That it is a language, more precisely a type of discourse rooted in a language, will likely prove controversial. To meet understandable objections that only by metaphor is "star-talk" a language, I have argued first that the ancients themselves, in particular the great Christian thinkers Origen and Augustine, frequently spoke of the visible heavens as the product of

133

inscription, literally understood as text written and read (Beck 2006: 164–89). For the Christians the question was, if God wrote the text, who or what were the intermediaries transmitting it to us humans, were they good or evil, are we capable of understanding the text, should we, may we try? Augustine returned the answer that astrology is devils' talk and that in speaking it the astrologer knowingly or unknowingly joins a thoroughly corrupt and corrupting language community. In his gentler, more nuanced way Origen suggests that the discourse of the stars is not intended for us fallen humans at all. Star-talk is the medium in which God both commands and entertains his angels.[1]

Secondly, I argued that the signs of star-talk function in their proper contexts in the same way as the signs of natural languages (Beck 2006: 153–64).[2] A natural language is a code – but a public one – with rules and conventions familiar to all its users, in which meaning is expressed and communicated by signs which themselves have agreed and stable meanings.

Consider the following:

Mars in Aquarius sends his antiscium into Scorpio.

It is a sentence in the English language, rendering the Latin sentence of Firmicus Maternus at the start of *Mathesis* 2.29.15. You may recognize it from chapter 7, section 3 as part of the horoscope of Ceionius Rufius Albinus. With your understanding of ancient astrology you now know what the sentence means, because you know what "Mars," "Aquarius," "antiscium," and "Scorpio" mean. You also know that an antiscium is something that can be "sent," and that if it is launched from Aquarius it will land in Scorpio. Lastly, you know that the sentence is properly formed and that it asserts a proposition which happens to be true, both synthetically in respect to the actual horoscope and analytically in that by definition an antiscium from Aquarius can only be sent into Scorpio (sent into any other sign it wouldn't be an antiscium).

Now consider this same sentence presented as a fact or an event:

Mars-in-Aquarius-sending-his-antiscium-into-Scorpio.

134

For the astrologer (and for us imagining ourselves in the ancient astrologer's shoes) comprehending the fact or event is just the beginning. For over and above its factuality, it is a *sign signifying* something, in this instance trouble, actual or potential, of a certain sort for Ceionius Rufius Albinus. More precisely, it is a bundle of signs, each with its own denotation, arranged syntactically, as words in a sentence, so as to convey a meaning over and above the meanings of the individual signs.

I want to side-step the obvious, very real, but in the present context secondary problem of the temporal relationship between the giving of the celestial sign and its terrestrial outcome. Here I am concerned with issues of language, not with issues of real time or real life, for my point is a limited one: that astrology is – or was – a beautiful and subtle construction of the human linguistic and semiotic imagination.

The peculiarity of star-talk is that its signs are envisioned as themselves the primary speakers and writers of the language. Either autonomously or at the behest of some higher power they inscribe the text which is actually nothing but the motions and ever-changing patterns of their dance. Astrologers and other human (or angelic or demonic) speakers merely replicate what they have heard or read in that dance, extending (or enhancing or perverting) the meanings they believe are intended there. Hence secondary star-talk, of which genethlialogy was the most developed form.

Ancient astrology rested on the widely held premise that the heavens are *meaningful*, in the literal sense of being *full of meaning*. Stars may or may not *cause*, but they surely do *signify*. So what do they signify? The philosopher Plotinus allowed that some part of that signifying might be directed at humans on earth, but we should not be so arrogant as to suppose that that was its primary intent:

> We must rather say that the movement of the stars is for the preservation of the universe, but that they perform in addition another service; this is that those who know how to read this sort of writing can, by looking at them as if they were letters, read the future from their patterns, discovering what is signified by the systematic use of analogy. (*Ennead* 3.1.6, trans. Armstrong)

135

For each [planetary god] has its own life to itself, and each one's good is in its own act, and has nothing to do with us. The action on us of living beings that have no part with us is always something incidental, not their dominant activity. As with birds, their acting as signs is incidental; their work is not directed at us at all. (*Ennead* 2.3.3, trans. Armstrong)

In this book I have set out to present and explicate something of star-talk's genethlialogical utterances in antiquity. If I have persuaded you to listen to and enjoy this imaginary and imaginative discourse, once of wide currency, I shall have succeeded.

Notes

Chapter 1

1   I do however acknowledge that while this paradigm may be fairly charac-
    terized as the currently dominant one it is in fact explicitly rejected by the
    series (Sciences of Antiquity) in which Tamsyn Barton's commendable
    study of ancient astrology (1994) appeared.
2   Terminology is never a reliable guide, for the words *astronomia* and
    astrologia could be used indiscriminately of either practice, as could
    astronomos and *astrologos* of the practitioners. A frequently used term for
    astrologer was "mathematician"!

Chapter 2

1   I follow David Pingree's (1995: 82) taxonomy of forms of astrology.
2   The original is more easily accessible and its context explicated in Bidez
    and Cumont 1938: II.182.
3   On Babylonian omen astrology see Reiner 1999.
4   The other solution is to junk the true lunar months and institute a purely
    solar calendar in which the "month" is merely an arbitrary twelfth (more
    or less) of the year. Our world-wide modern civil calendar is descended
    from the Roman calendar, as reformed by Julius Caesar in 46–45 BCE. The

nineteen-year Metonic cycle is named after Meton, an Athenian astronomer who discovered it (perhaps independently of the Babylonians) in or before 432 BCE. On the lunar (synodic) month and the luni-solar calendar in Babylon and elsewhere in the ancient world, see Bickerman 1968: 16–26; Neugebauer 1975: 353–7 (vol. 1); Hannah 2005: 83–5.

5 My description is of course a gross simplification, justified solely by the fact that astronomy, whether Greek or Babylonian, is not our topic. Those interested in Babylonian astronomy, both for its own sake and as the original matrix for Greek astrology, might want to look at the essays by A. A. Aaboe and A. Sachs in the 1974 collection *The Place of Astronomy in the Ancient World*, edited by F. R. Hodson; also at the essays in the 1999 collection *Ancient Astronomy and Celestial Divination*, edited by N. M. Swerdlow, in particular Swerdlow's Introduction and H. Hunger's essay. This collection also contains E. Reiner's essay on Babylonian omen astrology and F. Rochberg's on Babylonian horoscopes. The fundamental work on Babylonian mathematical astronomy is Book II in Vol. 1 of Otto Neugebauer's *History of Ancient Mathematical Astronomy* (1975).

6 Reiner 1999 contains several examples of Babylonian omen astrology as well as a discussion.

7 On Babylonian horoscopes see Rochberg 1998 and 1999. The former work is a collection of all Babylonian horoscopes known to date; the latter gives several examples and discusses in full the complicated question of the relationship of the horoscopes to the other categories of astronomical texts, both mathematical and nonmathematical.

8 Jones 1991: 443. The suggestion that Hipparchus himself fetched what he wanted was made by G. J. Toomer (1988).

9 The classic study of alien wisdom is the book of that title by A. Momigliano (1975).

10 Such works are called pseudepigrapha. On the pseudepigrapha attributed to the ancient Persian magi, "Zoroaster" included, see Bidez and Cumont 1938, Beck 1991.

11 The earliest observations cited in the *Almagest* (4.6) are a trio dating to 721–720 BCE.

12 The Greek sources for these speculations are given in Bidez and Cumont 1938: II.7–14.

13 473,000 years (Diodorus 2.31.9), 490,000 and 730,000 (Pliny, *Natural History* 7.56.193). Pliny at least gets the recording medium ("baked bricks") right.

14 Sextus Empiricus, *Against the Mathematicians* ("mathematician" was another word for astrologer) 5.105. Sextus' "great year" spanned 9,977 ordinary years.

15 Cicero, *On Divination* 2.46.97.

16 For more information on Nechepso and Petosiris see Barton 1994: 26–8.

17 On Hermetic literature and the culture from which it sprang see Fowden 1986.

18 The story is brilliantly retold and analyzed by J. Z. Smith (1978). The translations quoted here are his.

Chapter 3

1 The tropical month is virtually the same as the "sidereal" month which is the length of time it takes for the Moon to return to the same position relative to the fixed stars rather than to the tropic (i.e. tropic and equinoctial) points. The precession of the equinoxes, mentioned above, is responsible for the very slight difference.

2 Retrograde motion is an epiphenomenon caused by the earth's own motion. We observe the planets from a moving platform, which will cause other planets on occasions to *appear* to be moving backwards against the background of the fixed stars.

3 Jones 1994: 28–9, 38–9; 1999b: 302.

4 Jones 1999a: 42–44; 1999b: 324–8.

5 On the "centers" see Neugebauer and Van Hoesen 1959: 3; Bouché-Leclercq 1899: 257–9.

6 On the "climates" see Neugebauer and Van Hoesen 1959: 3–4; Neugebauer 1975: 725–36. Because of the obliquity of the ecliptic its signs take different lengths of time to rise and to set. Some are "fast-risers" and "slow-setters," others vice versa, and the relative durations vary with geographic latitude, although the *average* "rising time" is everywhere 2 hours (2 hours × 12 signs = 24 hours). On the matter of "rising times," see Neugebauer and Van Hoesen 1959: 11; Neugebauer 1975, 725–36; Bouché-Leclercq 1899: 257–69.

7 "Minus 3" indicates the date. In this system of dating, used by historians of astronomy, the zero year is 1 BCE, so −3 is the same as 4 BCE.

8 "Original" horoscopes in N&VH's terminology are self-contained documents, mostly scraps of papyrus, as opposed to "literary" horoscopes which are those embedded in ancient astrological literature. The two

types are catalogued separately in N&VH, the numbers for the latter being prefixed "L."

9   Since Mercury was then very close to the cusp of Virgo and Libra, it is impossible to say with certainty which of the two signs the astrologer did in fact select. It would probably depend on the table of sign-entry dates he was using.

10 I use, for example, Carina Software's Voyager II Dynamic Sky Simulator™.

11 With a rectilinear grid the distortion towards the poles of the ecliptic is considerable. At the actual poles (celestial latitudes + and −90°) what should be points are displayed as lines, namely the upper and lower boundaries of the chart. This is of no consequence since our concern is solely with the seven planets and the four cardinal points, all of which are on or close to the ecliptic (latitude 0°).

12 Horoscopes, as we saw above, are latitude-specific. Although this particular horoscope, like the great majority of papyrus horoscopes, came from Oxyrhynchus, the latitude of Alexandria may be assumed for any Egyptian horoscope.

13 For a more realistic view (which is what these programs are actually more interested in conveying) you must (1) switch to 180° projection, and (2) select the "altazimuth" mode of viewing. The latter will give you a naturalistic horizon in the lower half of the screen, from which you can scroll upwards towards the zenith. You can also pan to the right or left to look at the sky above different sectors of the horizon. Remember that if it's daytime what you "see" is invisible! If your interest is *ancient* astronomy and astrology, set the coordinate system and grid lines to celestial longitude and latitude (based on the ecliptic), not to right ascension and declination (based on the celestial equator).

14 Inevitably there will be slight differences in longitude between planetary data generated by different computational programs, whether electronic (such as that used here) or pre-electronic (such as that used by N&VH [see pp. 1–2]). Simply to find planetary (including solar and lunar) longitudes for the period 601 BCE to 1649 CE one may use the tables in the two volumes of Tuckerman 1962, interpolating for the five- and ten-day intervals.

15 See note 9, above.

16 Why the angular distance between the ascendant and midheaven is not 90° was explained in section 5, above. Almost certainly, the astrologer of our horoscope, who in any case nowhere gives the precise degree of a sign, assumed four equal quadrants.

Chapter 4

1 On good and bad aspects see Bouché-Leclercq 1899: 165–74.

2 On polarity and opposition in Greek thought see Lloyd 1966: 15–171.

3 On this topic see Bouché-Leclercq 1899: 273–88; Neugebauer and Van Hoesen 1959: 7–8 (under "Loci").

4 Alternatively from a point 5° or 15° ahead of the ascendant.

5 As this is the first significant reference to *CCAG*, let me explicate it in full: Volume 8, Part 3, page 116, line 32, to page 117, line 27. This is the summary of Antiochus' version. For the version of Thrasyllus, drawing explicitly on Hermes, see *CCAG* 8.3.101.16–30. Accessible in English translation are the discussions of the places in two Latin sources: Manilius (early first century CE), *Astronomica* 2.788–967 (trans. G. P. Goold in the Loeb edition); Firmicus Maternus (fourth century), *Mathesis* 2.14–20 (trans. Rhys Bram 1975: 43–52). Somewhat confusingly, Manilius also treats the twelve-sector fixed circle all over again in Book 3 (43–159) with different nomenclature (12 "tasks" rather than 12 "temples").

6 In Greek a *daimôn* is a spirit of some sort, intermediate between a god and a human. Each one of us has his or her own *daimôn*, which is like a projection of the person on to the supernatural plane. Astrology envisions one on the dark side, the Bad Daemon, and one on the light, the Good Daemon, respectively our guardian devil and our guardian angel.

7 Dorotheus I.5.1–2. Dorotheus' work survives in its entirety only in Arabic. David Pingree's edition has an English translation following the Arabic text (1976: 161–322). Fragments of the original also survive in quotation or paraphrase in later Greek astrologers (Pingree 1976: 323–427). For the present passage I have translated one of these fragments (1976: 325, cf. 164).

8 Manilius also offers a simplified form of the circle of places which divides it into four quadrants in clockwise order governing infancy, youth, maturity, and old age (2.841–55). Thus life begins and ends at the ascendant.

9 This is not to say that slaves can't have a horoscope, even if born into slavery. Both in principle and in practice they can. Remember too that many household slaves, especially those with a valuable skill and education, were far better off materially than the free proletariat.

10 Note however that the Roman poet Manilius uses the Roman technical augural term *templum* as a term for the astrological places (e.g. *Astronomica* 2.959). Incidentally, English has inherited two words with roughly similar

meanings from Roman augury/auspicy and Graeco-Roman astrology respectively: to "contemplate" and to "consider" (from the Latin *sidus* = "star"). On the augural *templum*, see Beck 1994: 336–7, 346–7.

Chapter 5

1 On the three squares see Bouché-Leclercq 1899: 152–3. The original intent of the term "double-bodied" as applied to this quartet of signs you will find not in Ptolemy but in (e.g.) Manilius, *Astronomica* 2.660–3.
2 Boll 1910: 16, 40–4. The Calendar of Filocalus (354 CE) also names December 25 the "birthday of the Unconquered" (sc. Sun). Whether or not the Christians co-opted this local Roman festival for Christmas is here immaterial. See Hijmans 2003 for a recent and persuasive case that they did not.
3 To be precise, in an ascending and descending spiral, thus combining daily motion westward with the alternating northward and southward bias of annual motion eastward.
4 From the Roman poet Catullus (5.4–6).
5 Antiochus' scheme is actually more complicated. This same quartering in terms of north/south and exaltation/humiliation can be applied to different quadrants of the zodiac depending on the planet chosen. The primary planet is of course the Sun, since the solar quadrants are tied to actualities in the real world. The quadrants formed by other planets as they move from south to north of the ecliptic (not the equator as with the Sun) are not the same as the seasonal solar quadrants. There is an additional complication in that the nodes of the lunar and other planetary orbits (i.e. the points where they intersect the ecliptic) are not fixed in the same way that the equinoxes are fixed. We shall meet the migrating lunar nodes in the guise of pseudo-planets in the next chapter.
6 On the qualities and elements see (e.g.) Lloyd 1966: 23–6.
7 Note the assumption: if the leader, then (obviously) male. We shall look at the gendering of the heavens in the next chapter when we discuss the anthropomorphic and thus necessarily gendered planets.
8 Manilius' reasons for the last are explained by G. P. Goold in his edition of the Astronomica (1977: xxxix).
9 The schemes are set out at their simplest by Ptolemy, *Tetr.* 1.15–16.
10 As an exercise in astrological logic, match the two sets of examples and determine whether the enmities are quite as arbitrary as Manilius suggests.

11　The constellation stories, which were usually of the "just-so" type, were collected by an author called Hyginus – there were several of that name in the first and second centuries CE – in a treatise which survives under the title *On Astronomy*. The work is accessible in English translation in Condos 1997. A compendious modern source is R. H. Allen's *Star Names: Their Lore and Meaning* (1963, reprint of 1899 edition).

12　In the ancient context, being born under (e.g.) Leo does not necessarily mean that the Sun was in Leo when you were born. It is just as likely to mean that you were born when Leo (with or without the Sun) was in the ascendant. The sources normally specify the particular meaning intended, thus avoiding the nebulous "under" or equivalent. "Influence," by the way, is another word from the astrological lexicon: it means that which "flows in" from the surrounding heavens.

13　I have taken these examples of leonine qualities from Gordon 1980: 5.32–7, 46–7. Richard Gordon's article concerns the use of ancient animal lore in Mithraism, a mystery cult in which the "Lions" were initiates at a certain stage in the hierarchy. Mithraism was permeated with astrology (in a broad sense), and the celestial Lion served, as it were, as a lens to focus the lore of terrestrial lions onto the Mithraic Lions.

14　As Manilius puts it, they "mock the sea with man-made shores at the bidding of luxury" (4.263). Moralists of the time considered such structures the epitome of that conspicuous consumerism and hubristic excess which "got us into trouble in the first place."

15　The classic study is Franz Cumont's *L'Égypte des astrologues* (1937).

16　Index under "natives, types of."

17　Interestingly, Trimalchio's mercantile activities fit Manilius' profile of Cancers (4.162–75) to a T. Otherwise, there is little match between expositions of Manilius and our home-spun "mathematician."

18　The ultimate work on the signs of the zodiac in literary sources is Hübner 1982 (in German – Latin and Greek untranslated); on the zodiac and its signs as represented visually, Gundel 1992 (text in German – beautifully and copiously illustrated).

Chapter 6

1　In any case we can tell that the Moon is the closest of the planets because occasionally it can be seen to pass in front of the Sun or any one of the other five. These are visible events which we call an "eclipse" of the Sun and an "occultation" of one of the other planets.

2 The argument for scientific neutrality I find somewhat anachronistic and unconvincing. More often than not, the descriptive names were used in conjunction with the theophoric names. Very occasionally the descriptive names were used in actual horoscopes (with or without the theophoric names), e.g. Neugebauer and Van Hoesen 1959, nos. 81, 176; Jones 1999a: nos. 4277, 4283.

3 There is a French translation of Book 1 of the *Anthologies* (Bara 1989).

4 With colds and dysentery and suchlike Valens includes spirit possession and (male) sexual pathologies. Astrological sources are ambivalent on whether Saturn is cold and wet or cold and dry, i.e. watery or earthy.

5 The reader has to supply the implicit link: wooly Aries is the astrological "house" of Mars.

6 I follow Barbara Lex's terminology (1979). Lex studies there the engagement of each side of the autonomous nervous system in religious activity and experience: meditation is trophotropic, fast-paced ritual ergotropic.

7 On Saturn as the "Star of the Sun" see Beck 1988: 86–8.

8 I highly recommend Plutarch's dialogue *On the Face in the Moon* (Cherniss 1968) as a fascinating exploration of a topic at the intersection of ancient astronomy, physics, philosophy, theology, and myth.

9 Even from a geocentric point of view, there are observable relationships between the Sun and all other planets individually. This cannot be said of any of the others.

10 On the narrative of the descent and return of the soul through the planetary spheres, see Culianu 1983: 48–51.

11 Narratives of this sort were understandably of particular interest to the mystery cult of Mithras, the Unconquered *Sun* (to give him his cult title), on which see Beck 1988: 73–100; 2006: 102–52.

12 Ptolemy's explanation of the sects (*Tetr.* 1.7) is an interesting feat of astrological rationalization.

13 Note that in modern astrology "houses" are what the ancients called "places" (on which see chapter 4, section 3).

14 The original Greek term *tapeinôma* denoted low status. I have avoided the customary translation "depression" because of its modern psychological connotations.

15 I have made a few omissions and have frequently parted company from
    N&VH's translation in word choice where the language is non-technical. In
    only one place, the final phrase for Mars, do I find a different sense. In
    N&VH the number of the horoscope is also its date. Hence no. 81 dates to
    81 CE. A minus sign indicates a date BCE, though remember that in this
    astronomical system, because the zero year is 1 BCE, −1 will be 2 BCE, −2
    will be 3 BCE, and so on. Horoscopes prefixed "L" are those embedded as
    examples in literary sources. Those without an "L" are original documents,
    mostly papyri. The category of "deluxe" horoscopes is used in Jones'
    collection (1999a).

16 In other words between 8:00 and 9:00 p.m. on March 31, 81 CE, by our
    reckoning. Since the Roman day began at sunset on the evening before, the
    Kalends (first) of April had already arrived when birth occurred.

17 Unusually, this horoscope describes, here and elsewhere, the actual position
    of the planet in the constellation as well as its longitude in the sign.

18 On the *dodekatemoria* see above, chapter 5, section 9.

19 *Anabibazousa* is the feminine form of the participle of a Greek verb
    meaning "to cause to ascend," here used intransitively in the sense of
    simply "ascending." This would be entirely unremarkable were it not that
    the masculine form *anabibazôn* happens to be the technical term for the
    ascending node of the Moon's orbit, the point at which she crosses from
    south to north of the ecliptic (the point at which she crosses back again
    from north to south, the descending node, was called *katabibazôn*). Is the
    astrologer indicating more than the position and motion of the Moon in
    the constellation of Taurus: that the Moon is also going north in the
    ascending semicircle of her orbit? If so, he is wrong, for the Moon was at
    the time going south after crossing the ecliptic at the descending node
    some five days before. In later Greek astrology the two nodes, whose
    positions on the ecliptic change over time, were co-opted as an eighth
    and a ninth planet whose locations and astrological intent could be in-
    cluded in a horoscope. Students of the Mithras cult will find the phrase
    "mounting the back of Taurus the Bull" quite evocative, for that is what the
    cult icon shows Mithras doing. Moreover, the astrological "meanings" of
    the Bull in the icon are both "Moon" and "Taurus" (Beck 2006: 194–200).
    In the same study (206–7) I argue that the torchbearers Cautes (raised
    torch) and Cautopates (lowered torch) "mean," among other pairs of
    celestial opposites, Anabibazon and Katabibazon.

20 Saturn was then 38° to the east of the Sun and so could be seen rising ahead of him in the pre-dawn (morning) twilight.

21 By "Swallow-Fish" the more northerly of the two fishes of Pisces is probably intended (see N&VH pp. 26–7), though actually Saturn was then closer to the more southerly.

22 Aquarius, the Water-Carrier, was sometimes identified with, and therefore called, Ganymede. Ganymede was a beautiful boy, kidnapped by Zeus/Jupiter to be his personal cup-bearer.

23 Actually Venus was then closer to the more northerly of the two Fishes.

24 By "having completed its phase before the seventh" the astrologer means that on the next day, Pharmouthi the seventh, Mercury will have completed his phase as a morning star rising ahead of the Sun. He will then be in (superior) conjunction with the Sun, from which fact the astrologer infers his predominance over the other planets in the horoscope.

25 On the "lots" see the appendix to the present chapter.

26 On these "perpetual tables" see N&VH p. 24, Toomer 1984: 422, n. 12. They are mentioned somewhat dismissively by Ptolemy, *Almagest* 9.2. None has survived.

Chapter 7

1 Not 188, which Pingree (1986: vi, n. 1) redates to 70 CE.

2 A Roman numeral is used to distinguish horoscopes of the same year by month. Thus L113.IV dates to April 113. When two horoscopes fall in the same month, the day of the month is appended in Arabic numerals: e.g. L122.I.30.

3 This horoscope also happens to be the only horoscope of a real person in all of the extant Latin astrological literature (which means in effect Firmicus and Manilius).

4 The antiscium is required because without it the Moon would not be in any aspect to Mars. The lunar antiscium in Gemini is in trine aspect to Mars (good for Mars, bad for the Moon).

5 Sympathetic treatments by M. T. Riley (1996) and J. Komorowska (2004).

6 For chapter numbers in Valens, I follow Pingree's edition (1986) rather than those used by N&VH which were based on W. Kroll's earlier edition.

7 On rising times and the climata, see N&VH, pp. 3–5, 11.

8 See the commentaries on the individual horoscopes in N&VH; also pp. 182–4.

9 Chapter 11 of Book 4 is of particular interest because it is prefaced by a long autobiographical passage in which Valens is at pains to promote the value of the procedure and to assert his own intellectual property rights over it.

10 The phrase makes no sense as it stands. Perhaps it is an interpolation.

11 The heliacal rising of Sirius, i.e. the first day in the year when it can be seen rising ahead of the sun in the pre-dawn twilight, was a datum used in ancient astrology from the earliest times. See above, chapter 2, section 1.

12 Noting that Mars was in Virgo is not an essential step in the procedure, though it does put Virgo in a properly sinister light.

13 The reason for "subtracting twelves" and working with the remainder should now be clear. Since the twelve signs repeat themselves in the same order, counting off eleven signs achieves the same result as counting off 203 – and is a lot quicker.

14 Equally extraordinary is that the implied clima, i.e. geographic latitude, appears to be no. 5. That would seem to imply Byzantium/Constantinople, which is actually midway between nos. 5 and 6 (on contradictions in the implied clima see N&VH's commentary on the horoscope). Though reasonable as the site for the imagined consultation in the year 621, it is absurd as the clima for the nation whose astonishing rise the horoscope predicts.

15 In fact zygon/zygos is cognate both with English "yoke" and with Latin iugum. The latter gives us the English compound "sub-jug-ation."

16 N&VH omit from their translation the twelve lines of the horoscope (274.5–16) which discuss Venus' influence on the Arab/Muslim character. Abstinence from wine is also mentioned.

17 Mercury's location is not given in the text but only in the two manuscript diagrams. Its longitude in one diagram is identical to the Sun's (Virgo 9° 5′), which is probably an error, since its actual longitude was Virgo 27°.

Chapter 8

1 Note however Bouché-Leclerq's caution: "To suppose that once the point of departure and the point of arrival were fixed the calculation of the length of life could be reduced simply to a measurement of the arc between these

two points would be seriously to misunderstand the spirit of Greek astrology" (1899: 420, my translation).

2   Even the great Ptolemy is not exempt from Bouché-Leclerq's strictures: "I do not intend to force my way any further into the maze of exceptions, adjustments, and alternative procedures which Ptolemy accumulates with the detached air of a man who seems to want to render the problem insoluble rather than to teach the means of solving it" (1899: 122, my translation).

3   My translation follows all the N&VH emendations to the text but does not adhere to the wording of their translation.

4   This step is not without parallel. One quadrant of ninety degrees/years is more or less the limit for a ripe old age, not four quadrants totaling three-hundred-and-sixty degrees/years.

5   Firmicus subsequently converted to Christianity and wrote a polemical work entitled *On the Error of the Profane Religions*.

6   Antigonus does not name Hadrian. The emperor's identity had to be worked out from the horoscope's date and the native's biography.

7   On the "terms" see above, chapter 6, section 7.

8   Even so, there remains the problem of why this royal star was located at Aquarius 22°, when its position was known to be well to the west, at Aquarius 7° in Ptolemy's catalogue. However, there is no possible alternative since Formalhaut is the only first-magnitude star in this rather dim tract of the heavens.

9   And more succinctly by Tamsyn Barton in her *Ancient Astrology* (1994: 32–52). The astrologers make an appropriate appearance among the "enemies of the Roman order" in Ramsay MacMullen's excellent book of that title (1966: 128–42).

10 On Thrasyllus see Cramer 1954: 92–5, 99–108; on Balbillus, Cramer 1954: 112–14, 118, 126–8, 135–9. The precise biographies and the family tree of the two men still pose some problems, on which see Beck 1998: 126–7.

11 Our sources for first-century CE history were neither naive nor especially credulous. For the stories about astrologers in high politics they are the historians Tacitus (writing at the beginning of the second century) and Cassius Dio (early third century), the biographer of the first twelve "Caesars," Suetonius (early second century), and for the matter of Ennia Thrasylla, Caius Caesar and Macro, their contemporary Philo of Alexandria.

12   The episode is well discussed from all angles (historical, astronomical, astrological) by Pierre Brind'Amour (1981).

13   Thrasyllus composed a *Pinax to Hierocles* (a *pinax* is literally a writing tablet), the surviving summary of which was published in *CCAG* 8.3.99–101 (also in Tarrant 1993: 244–6). Balbillus wrote *Astrologumena to Hermogenes*: surviving summary in *CCAG* 8.3.103–4; excerpt containing the two horoscopes in *CCAG* 8.4.235–8. The addressee of the work may well be the Hermogenes of Tarsus who was put to death and his slave copyists crucified by Domitian "on account of certain figures (figures of speech? allusions? astrological diagrams?) in a "history" (Suetonius, *Domitian* 10.1). If that is so, Balbillus' work on length of life proved a poisoned chalice to his friend and his friend's household.

14   On Balbillus' marriage connection with the dynasty of Commagene see Beck 1998: 126–7. Some earlier scholars, including Cramer, took the view that Thrasyllus himself had married a Commagenian princess. On the astrology of Commagene and its legacy in the Roman cult of Mithras I have written much. To do the topic proper justice here would make this book half as long again, so I will simply refer the reader to my relevant publications: Beck 1998; 1999; 2004: 323–9; 2006: 227–39, 252–6.

Chapter 9

1   For a comprehensive study of early Christians attitudes to astrology see the forthcoming (2006) book by Timothy Hegedus.

2   In my study I argued that the astral symbolism of the so-called Mysteries of Mithras functioned as a language. In particular I made the case for an exception to Dan Sperber's general principle (1975), with which I am in agreement, that symbols do not "mean" in the way language signs "mean." Rather, they "evoke" or, as the ancients would say, "intimate" (*ainitesthai*, whence our word "enigma").

References

Aaboe, A. 1974: Scientific astronomy in antiquity. In Hodson, 21–42.

Allen, R. H. 1963: *Star Names: Their Lore and Meaning.* New York: Dover. [Reprint of 1899 edition entitled *Star-Names and Their Meanings.*]

Barton, T. 1994: *Ancient Astrology.* London and New York: Routledge.

Bara, J.-F. (ed. and trans.) 1989: *Vettius Valens d'Antioche: Anthologies, Livre I.* Leiden: Brill.

Beck, R. L. 1988: *Planetary Gods and Planetary Orders in the Mysteries of Mithras.* Leiden: Brill.

—— 1991: Thus spake not Zarathustra: Zoroastrian pseudepigrapha in the Greco-Roman world. An excursus in M. Boyce and F. Grenet, *A History of Zoroastrianism,* vol. 3. Leiden: Brill, 491–565.

—— 1994: Cosmic models: Some uses of Hellenistic science in Roman religion. In T. D. Barnes (ed.), *The Sciences in Greco-Roman Society, Apeiron* 26 (4). Edmonton: Academic Printing and Publishing, 99–117. Reprinted as chapter 16 in Beck 2004: 335–53.

—— 1998: The mysteries of Mithras: A new account of their genesis. *Journal of Roman Studies* 88:115–28. Reprinted as chapter 2 in Beck 2004: 31–44.

—— 1999: The astronomical design of Karakush, a royal burial site in ancient Commagene: An hypothesis. *Culture and Cosmos* 3 (1):10–34. Reprinted as chapter 14 in Beck 2004: 297–321.

—— 2004: *Beck on Mithraism: Collected Works with New Essays*. Ashgate Contemporary Thinkers on Religion: Collected Works. Aldershot (UK) and Burlington, VT: Ashgate Publishing.

—— 2006: *The Religion of the Mithras Cult in the Roman Empire: Mysteries of the Unconquered Sun*. Oxford: Oxford University Press.

Bickerman, E. J. 1968: *Chronology of the Ancient World*. London: Thames and Hudson.

Bidez, J. and Cumont, F. 1938 [reprint 1973]: *Les mages hellénisés: Zoroastre, Ostanès et Hystaspe d'après la tradition grecque*. Vol. I, *Introduction*. Vol. II, *Les textes*. Paris: Les Belles Lettres.

Boll, F. 1910: *Griechische Kalender: 1. Das Kalendarium des Antiochos*. Sitzungsberichte der Heidelberger Akademie der Wissenschaften, philos.-hist. Klasse, Jahrgang 1910, 16. Abhandlung. Heidelberg: Carl Winter's Universitätsbuchhandlung.

Bouché-Leclercq, A. 1899 [1963]: *L'Astrologie grecque*. Paris [reprint Brussels: Culture et Civilisation].

Brind'Amour, P. 1981: Problèmes astrologiques et astronomiques soulevés par le récit de la mort de Domitien chez Suétone. *Phoenix* 35:338–44.

CCAG = (various editors) 1898–1953: *Catalogus Codicum Astrologorum Graecorum*, 12 vols. in 20 parts. Brussels: Lamertin.

Cherniss, H. (ed. and trans.) 1968: *Plutarch's Moralia XII*. Loeb Classical Library. Cambridge MA and London: Harvard University Press and Heinemann.

Condos, T. 1997: *Star Myths of the Greeks and Romans: A Sourcebook, Containing* The Constellations *of Pseudo-Eratosthenes and the* Poetic Astronomy *of Hyginus*. Grand Rapids: Phanes Press.

Cramer, F. H. 1954: *Astrology in Roman Law and Politics*. Memoirs of the American Philosophical Society 37. Philadelphia: American Philosophical Society.

Culver, R. B. and Ianna, P. A. 1977: Astrology and the scientific method. *Astronomical Quarterly* 1:85–110, 147–72.

Culianu, I. P. 1983: *Psychanodia I*. Leiden: Brill.

Cumont, F. 1935: Les noms des planètes et l'astrolatrie chez les Grecs. *L'Antiquité Classique* 4:5–43.

—— 1937 [1982]: *L'Égypte des astrologues*. Brussels: Fondation Égyptologique Reine Elisabeth. [Reprint Brussels: Éditions Culture et Civilisation.]

Dorotheus of Sidon, *Carmen astrologicum*: see Pingree 1976.

151

Firmicus Maternus, *Mathesis*: see Rhys Bram 1975.

Fowden, G. 1986: *The Egyptian Hermes: A Historical Approach to the Late Pagan Mind*. Cambridge: Cambridge University Press.

Geertz, C. 1973: *The Interpretation of Cultures: Selected Essays*. New York: Basic Books.

Goold, G. P. (ed. and trans.) 1977: *Manilius* Astronomica. Loeb Classical Library. Cambridge MA and London: Harvard University Press and Heinemann.

Gordon, R. L. 1980: Reality, evocation and boundary in the Mysteries of Mithras. *Journal of Mithraic Studies* 3:19–99. [Reprinted as chapter V in R. L. Gordon, *Image and Value in the Graeco-Roman World*. Variorum Collected Studies Series CS551. Aldershot: Ashgate Publishing, 1996.]

Gundel, H. G. 1992: *Zodiakos: Tierkreisbilder im Altertum. Kosmische Bezüge und Jenseitsvorstellungen im antiken Alltagsleben*. Kulturgeschichte der antiken Welt, Band 54. Mainz: Verlag Philipp von Zabern.

Gundel, W. and H. G. 1966: *Astrologumena: Die astrologische Literatur in der Antike und ihre Geschichte*. Sudhoffs Archiv, Beiheft 6. Wiesbaden: Franz Steiner Verlag.

Hannah, R. 2005: *Greek and Roman Calendars: Constructions of Time in the Classical World*. London: Duckworth.

Hegedus, T. M. J. Forthcoming: *Attitudes to Astrology in Early Christianity*. New York: Peter Lang.

Hephaestion, *Apotelematica*: see Pingree 1973.

Hijmans, S. 2003: Sol Invictus, the winter solstice, and the origins of Christmas. *Mouseion*, Series III, 3:377–98.

Hodson, F. R. (ed.) 1974: *The Place of Astronomy in the Ancient World*. London: Oxford University Press.

Hübner, W. 1982: *Die Eigenschaften der Tierkreiszeichen in der Antike*. Sudhoffs Archiv, Zeitschrift für Wissenschaftsgeschichte 22. Wiesbaden: Franz Steiner Verlag.

Hunger, H. 1999: Non-mathematical astronomical texts and their relationships. In Swerdlow, 77–96.

Hyginus, *On Astronomy*: see Condos 1997.

Jones, A. 1991: The adaptation of Babylonian methods in Greek numerical astronomy. *Isis* 82:441–53.

—— 1994: The place of astronomy in Roman Egypt. In T. D. Barnes (ed.), *The Sciences in Greco-Roman Society, Apeiron* 26 (4). Edmonton: Academic Printing and Publishing, 25–51.

—— 1999a: *Astronomical Papyri from Oxyrhynchus*. Memoirs of the American Philosophical Society 233. Philadelphia: American Philosophical Society.

—— 1999b: A classification of astronomical tables on papyrus. In Swerdlow, 299–340.

Komorowska, J. 2004: *Vettius Valens of Antioch: An Intellectual Monography*. Krakow: Ksiegarnia Akademicka.

Lex, B. W. 1979. The neurobiology of ritual trance. In E. G. d'Aquili, C. D. Laughlin, and J. McManus (eds), *The Spectrum of Ritual*. New York: Columbia University Press, 117–51.

Lloyd, G. E. R. 1966: *Polarity and Analogy: Two Types of Argumentation in Early Greek Thought*. Cambridge: Cambridge University Press.

Long, A. A. 1982: Astrology: Arguments pro and contra. In J. Barnes et al., *Science and Speculation: Studies in Hellenistic Theory and Practice*. Cambridge: Cambridge University Press, 165–92.

MacMullen, R. 1966 [1992]: *Enemies of the Roman Order: Treason, Unrest, and Alienation in the Empire*. Cambridge MA: Harvard University Press [Reprint London and New York: Routledge].

Manilius, *Astronomica*. see Goold 1977.

Momigliano, A. 1975 [reprint 1990]: *Alien Wisdom: The Limits of Hellenization*. Cambridge: Cambridge University Press.

Neugebauer, O. 1953: The horoscope of Ceionius Rufius Albinus. *American Journal of Philology* 74:418–20.

—— 1975: *A History of Ancient Mathematical Astronomy*. 3 vols. with consecutive pagination. Berlin, Heidelberg, New York: Springer Verlag.

Neugebauer, O. and Van Hoesen, H. B. 1959 (abbreviated N&VH): *Greek Horoscopes*. Memoirs of the American Philosophical Society 48. Philadelphia: American Philosophical Society.

Parker, R. A. 1974: Ancient Egyptian astronomy. In Hodson, 51–65.

Pingree, D. (ed.) 1973: *Hephaestionis Thebani Apotelesmaticorum Libri Tres*. 2 vols. Leipzig: Teubner.

—— (ed.) 1976: *Dorothei Sidonii Carmen Astrologicum*. Leipzig: Teubner.

—— (ed.) 1986: *Vettii Valentis Antiocheni Anthologiarum libri novem*. Leipzig: Teubner.

—— 1995: Astrology. *Encyclopaedia Britannica*, 15th edn., vol. 25, 81–5.

Plutarch, *On the Face in the Moon*: see Cherniss 1968.

Ptolemy, *Almagest*: see Toomer 1984.

—— *Tetrabiblos*: see Robbins 1971.

Reiner, E. 1999: Babylonian celestial divination. In Swerdlow, 21–37.

Rhys Bram, J. (trans.) 1975: *Ancient Astrology: Theory and Practice. The* Mathesis *of Firmicus Maternus.* Park Ridge, NJ: Noyes Press.

Riley, M. T. 1996: A survey of Vettius Valens. www.csus.edu/indiv/r/rileymt/ (accessed December 2005).

Robbins, F. E. (trans.) 1971: *Ptolemy: Tetrabiblos.* Loeb Classical Library. Cambridge MA and London: Harvard University Press and Heinemann.

Rochberg-Halton, F. 1988: Elements of the Babylonian contribution to Hellenistic astrology. *Journal of the American Oriental Society* 108:51–62.

Rochberg, F. 1998: *Babylonian Horoscopes.* Transactions of the American Philosophical Society, 88 (Pt. 1). Philadelphia: American Philosophical Society.

—— 1999: Babylonian horoscopy: The texts and their relations. In Swerdlow, 39–59.

Sachs, A. 1974: Babylonian observational astronomy. In Hodson, 43–50.

Smith, J. Z. 1978: The temple and the magician. In *Map is not Territory.* Leiden: Brill, 172–89.

Sperber, D. 1975: *Rethinking Symbolism.* Trans. A. L. Morton. Cambridge: Cambridge University Press.

Stahl, W. H. (trans.) 1952: *Macrobius: Commentary on the Dream of Scipio.* New York: Columbia University Press.

Swerdlow, N. M. (ed.) 1999: *Ancient Astronomy and Celestial Divination.* Cambridge, MA: MIT Press.

Tarrant, H. 1993: *Thrasyllan Platonism.* Ithaca: Cornell University Press.

Toomer, G. J. (trans.) 1984: *Ptolemy's Almagest.* London: Duckworth.

—— 1988: Hipparchus and Babylonian astronomy. In E. Leichty et al. (eds), *A Scientific Humanist: Studies in Memory of Abraham Sachs.* Philadelphia: American Philosophical Society, 353–62.

Tuckerman, B. 1962: *Planetary, Lunar, and Solar Positions.* Vol. 1, *601* BC *to* AD *1.* Vol. 2, AD *2 to* AD *1649.* Memoirs of the American Philosophical Society, 56. Philadelphia: American Philosophical Society.

Usener, H. 1965 [reprint of 1912–13 edition]: *Kleine Schriften.* Vol. 3. Osnabrück: Otto Zeller.

Vettius Valens, *Anthologies*: see Pingree 1986, Bara 1989.

Index